Driving Machines

The BMW Story

By

James Taylor

First published in 2000 by
Unity Media plc
Stakes House
Quebec Square
Westerham
Kent TN16 1UN
England

**British Library Cataloguing-
in-Publication Data**
A catalogue record of this
book is available from the
British Library

ISBN 0-9538309-0-X

Repro by Topscan Limited
Redhill
Surrey

Printed by:
Acorn Web Offset Limited
Normanton
West Yorkshire

Driving Machines

CONTENTS

Chapter 1   In The Beginning

Chapter 2   Growing Up, 1932-1936

Chapter 3   International Acclaim, 1936-1941

Chapter 4   War And Its Aftermath

Chapter 5   Back In Action

Chapter 6   The Sublime And The (Faintly) Ridiculous

Chapter 7   New And Classy

Chapter 8   Six For Success

Chapter 9   Fives And Threes

Chapter 10   Power, Prestige And Performance

Chapter 11   Symbols Of Their Times

Chapter 12   Today And Tomorrow

* *

Appendix A   The BMW Group

Appendix B   BMW's E-Series Codes

Appendix C   BMW Engines Since 1961: A Concordance

The early, pre-BMW Dixi looks almost identical to its close British cousin, the Austin Seven

Driving Machines

Chapter 1
IN THE BEGINNING

To find the origins of the BMW company, we have to go right back to 1913. That was the year when Karl Friedrich Rapp, a distinguished engineer who had been a director of an early German aircraft company, set up in business independently to manufacture aero engines. He established his new company, the Rapp Motoren Werke, in the Milbertshofen suburb of Munich, capital city of Bavaria. His choice of Munich was made primarily because one of his major customers – the Gustav Otto aircraft company - was situated nearby.

Rapp's own aero engines were a success, but he continued to look around for more work to keep his company busy. In 1916, he secured a contract to build a large number of V12 aero engines on behalf of Austro-Daimler, who were finding that they could not build enough to meet escalating demand. Rapp sought a backer to finance his company's expansion to meet this new challenge, and in March 1916 the Rapp Motoren Werke was renamed the Bayerische Motoren Werke. BMW - the Bavarian Engine Company - had been formed.

Unfortunately, Rapp had made the mistake of expanding his company too fast. Within a year, there were problems. Rapp himself left the company quickly, and in his place came the industrial tycoon Franz Josef Popp. It was Popp who laid the foundations of the company we know today.

The aero engines

The first aero engine to wear the BMW name was the Type IIIA, introduced in 1917. Designed by the company's chief engineer, Max Friz, it was a six-cylinder in-line engine which gave 185bhp. The first operational unit to receive BMW-powered biplanes was none other than the one commanded by Baron von Richthofen, the famous 'Red Baron'.

By 1919, Friz had developed the engine further into the Type IV, a larger-capacity engine which gave 250bhp (and was later rated as high as 320bhp). This set a new altitude record during 1919, though the BMW claim was never officially ratified. Type IV production was suspended by the Allied Control Commission, but resumed in 1925, and at the same time BMW also introduced a new Friz design. This was the Type VI, a 700bhp V12 which remained in production until 1939.

Left, BMW's first aero engine was the Type IIIA of 1917. It was developed further as the Type IV of 1919 (above)

The BMW Story

The motor cycle connection

When the Great War ended, BMW found itself in difficulties. The company had relied upon the manufacture of aircraft engines for their very existence, and more specifically had relied upon the manufacture of aero engines for warplanes. Under the Allied Control Commission which was set up in Germany after the War, the manufacture of war material of any kind was forbidden - and there was precious little demand for civilian aero engines at this stage.

As a temporary expedient, BMW secured a contract to make compressed-air brakes for railway trains on behalf of the Knorr company. But it was chief engineer Max Friz who saved the day. He redeveloped his own Type IIIA six-cylinder aero engine as a truck engine, and in due course the so-called 'Bayern Motor' found marine and industrial applications as well. Meanwhile, company chief Franz Josef Popp had decided that the company should safeguard its future by diversifying further - and he saw a step into motorcycle manufacture as the best way forward.

The versatile Friz was persuaded to design a new motorcycle, and by 1923 the BMW R-32 was ready to go into production in a

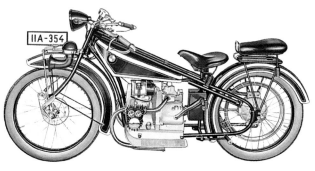

The 1923 R-32 was BMW's first motorcycle

second Munich factory recently acquired from another aircraft company which had fallen on hard times. The R-32 was a remarkably advanced design for its time, and one which would set the standard for 500cc machines for many years. Indeed, elements of its design are still to be seen in modern BMW motorcycles.

The key features of the R-32 were its sprung front wheel (a world first), its flat-twin engine, installed transversely in the frame to give equal cooling to both cylinders, and its shaft drive to the rear wheel. Friz had wisely decided not to use bevel gears to turn the drive from the crankshaft through 90 degrees as would have been necessary with conventional chain-drive; instead, he had chosen a simpler and mechanically more reliable shaft which took the drive directly to the rear wheel, where a pinion meshed with a ring gear in the wheel hub.

Brilliantly effective, the R-32 inspired several other BMW designs in the 1920s and 1930s. And BMW motorcycles swept the board in both national and international sporting events. Between 1923 and 1928 alone, they racked up an impressive 573 wins in major events.

The R-32 established the company's style with its twin-cylinder engine and shaft drive

Driving Machines

BMW's first car - the 3/15

So by the time BMW put its name to a car in 1928, it was already well established as one of the leading German industrial concerns. Since 1922, its growth had been spectacular, and its reputation was second to none in the aero engine and motor cycle fields where it operated during the Roaring Twenties.

The story of how the company came to make a car at all certainly bears telling. Inspired by the company's increasing success during the first half of the 1920s, BMW's head Franz Josef Popp started to look at ways of expanding its manufacturing interests some time around 1925 - and it seemed to him that cars would be a logical addition to the BMW product range.

These were times of rampant inflation in Germany, however. The effects of the 1914-1918 Great War were still being felt, and any attempt to sell luxury cars was likely to be doomed to failure. So Popp began by considering a revolutionary economy-car prototype designed by Professor Wunibald Kamm (the same Kamm later responsible for the aerodynamic 'Kamm tail'). This car was astonishingly advanced for its time, with chassisless aluminium alloy construction, front wheel drive, all-round independent suspension and a flat-twin engine - but it was also too complicated to be built cheaply. Popp therefore decided to look elsewhere.

Not long afterwards, towards the end of 1927, a new economy car appeared on the German market. Badged as the Dixi 3/15, it was actually the British-designed Austin Seven built under licence at a factory in Eisenach. As it happened, Popp knew the owner of the industrial group to which Dixi belonged, and he lost no time in proposing a deal under which the company and its manufacturing licences should pass to BMW. And so in September 1928, BMW bought Dixi, and the blue and white roundel began to appear on a car which was now called the BMW 3/15.

Design modifications, initially minor, soon began to make the 3/15 a very different car from its Austin relative, and by the time it went out of production in 1932 it was almost as much the work of BMW's chief engineer Max Friz as it was of Sir Herbert Austin. It was no fault of BMW's that sales had dropped off after the Great Depression of 1930, and that BMW managed to build only 19,000 3/15s in four years while Dixi had managed to sell 9,000 in one year during more prosperous times.

Throughout the period of 3/15 production, the car was built at the old Dixi plant in Eisenach. BMW headquarters nevertheless remained in Munich, some 200 miles away to the south. This was where the company had been established in 1916, and it was here that aero engines and motor cycles continued to be built. For the time being, it was an arrangement which worked well. But a decade and a half later, BMW was to regret bitterly that its main factories were so far apart as the Eisenach plant fell into Soviet hands in the eastern sector of a divided Germany.

The BMW Story

The 3/15 was recognisably related to the Austin Seven, but BMW had already started to make its mark on the car by the time of this DA-2 model

Driving Machines

The BMW Story

Open-air motoring was the style of the times, and convertible versions of the 3/15 (above) were popular. Even the saloon model (below) could have a folding roof

THE BLUE AND WHITE ROUNDEL

BMW's distinctive blue and white roundel badge was drawn up in the company's early days as an aero engine manufacturer. Look closely, and you can see why. The four coloured quadrants are a stylised representation of an aircraft propeller spinning (the white segments) against the background of a clear blue sky.

Driving Machines

BMW 3/15, types DA-1 to DA-4 (1928-1932)

The BMW (née Dixi) 3/15 was one of several licence-built versions of the Austin Seven, which was also manufactured by Datsun (Japan), Rosengart (France) and the American Austin Co. (USA). In four years of production, BMW built 18,976 examples of the car.

The 3/15's DA type designation was taken over from Dixi, whose first model was called the DA-1 (the letters stood for Deutsche Ausführung, or German Edition of the Austin Seven). However, BMW's own DA-1 differed from the Dixi version in several respects. Most notably, BMW had its bodies made by Ambi-Budd in Berlin; the Dixi bodies had been made by Mercedes-Benz in Sindelfingen.

The variants

Type DA-1	1928-1929	All-steel saloon body
Type DA-2	1929-1930	Saloon, two-seater convertible and delivery van
		Footbrake operated on all four wheels
		Lower final drive gearing
		Bigger wheels and tyres
Type DA-3	1930	Roadster only, known as the Wartburg. High-compression engine and drop-centre front axle
Type DA-4	1931-1932	Saloon, convertible and coupé
		Independent front suspension

Specification

Engine:	748cc (56 x 76.2mm) side-valve four-cylinder, with 5.6:1 compression ratio and 15bhp at 3000rpm (DA-3 model had 7:1 compression and 18bhp at 3500rpm).
Transmission:	Three-speed manual with reverse.
Axle ratio:	4.9:1 (DA-1); 5.35:1 (DA-2 to DA-4).
Front suspension:	Beam axle with transverse leaf spring (DA-1 to DA-3 models); independent front suspension with leading arms and transverse leaf spring (DA-4 models).
Rear suspension:	Beam axle with quarter-elliptic leaf springs.
Steering:	Worm and peg.
Brakes:	Drums all round; footbrake operated rear brakes only on DA-1 models.
Wheels and tyres:	26-inch wheels with 3in wide tyres (DA-1) 27-inch wheels with 4in wide tyres (DA-2 to DA-4).
Wheelbase:	75in
Overall length:	152in
Width:	63in
Weight:	1036-1179 lb. (470-535kg), depending on model; DA-3, 882 lb. (400kg).

The BMW Story

*The long-nose/short-body look of the
303 and 309 models is clear in this
view of a six-cylinder 303 cabriolet
from 1933-34*

Driving Machines

Chapter 2
GROWING UP, 1932-1936

With the little 3/15 model which it had taken over from Dixi in 1928, BMW made a successful entry to the car market. But these were hard times in Germany, and the Depression of the early 1930s was just around the corner. By the beginning of 1932, things were looking bad. BMW's capital stock, once as high as 16 million Reichmarks, had been written down to just 1 million; cash reserves were seriously depleted; and the bank insisted on putting a representative on the BMW supervisory board. The man they chose was Wilhelm Kissel, then Chairman of Daimler-Benz.

Distinctively BMW's own: the 3/20 type AM-4

Although car sales did begin to pick up towards the middle of the decade, it was not car production which kept BMW afloat. Rather it was the well-established motor cycle and aero engine sides of the business. Motor cycles were selling around 10,000 a year, and the aero engine business increased considerably when Germany began to re-arm after Hitler's rise to power in 1933.

Yet BMW Chairman Franz Josef Popp was insistent that the car side of the business should not founder. The contract with Austin to build its Seven under licence as the BMW 3/15 expired in March 1932, and long before that date Popp was planning to build an all-BMW car. However, the proposals which chief engineer Max Friz came up with during 1931 were not what he wanted, and in the end Friz resigned. His place

was taken by Alfred Böning as chief designer.

Böning was given a matter of months to get a new model ready for the autumn of 1931. To his credit, he succeeded, and the new BMW 3/20 (which was really a redeveloped, all-BMW, 3/15) went on sale for the 1932 model-year alongside the last of the old models. This was a step in the right direction, but Popp wanted more - a bigger car with better performance. So a year later came the 303, a class above the 3/20 in size. Most important, this car had a six-cylinder engine, and was the cheapest 'six' on sale in Germany at the time. While it had its faults, particularly in the suspension design, it showed BMW the way ahead.

The 3/20 disappeared a year after that, to be replaced from the autumn of 1933 by the four-cylinder 309, itself a 303 derivative. And at the same time, BMW expanded its six-cylinder range by introducing a pair of larger-capacity engines in the 315 and 319. So by 1935, the BMW range started with the four-cylinder 309, progressed to the 303 'small six', and went through the intermediate 315 to the top-model 319. From that year, rakish roadster versions of the 315 and 319 were also made available, and took advantage of the vastly improved chassis design of these later cars as well as their more powerful engines.

A 315 cabriolet from the mid-1930s

Stolid six: the 319, built from 1935 to 1937

But another new era was just beginning, for it was in 1935 that BMW unveiled its redesigned 2-litre 'six', the engine which would create a legend.

The four-cylinder cars: 3/20 and 309

The main failing of the 3/15 was its lack of interior space, and Franz Josef Popp instructed Alfred Böning to create a larger successor. Böning stretched the wheelbase by nearly 11 inches and, although the chassis still carried echoes of Austin practice in its A-shaped layout, he gave it tubular side-members for greater rigidity. He also added the BMW-designed independent front suspension seen on the last DA-4 models of the 3/15, and then went one step further by designing an independent rear suspension - advanced thinking for the early 1930s.

The engine, too, was Austin-derived. Starting with the 747cc Austin unit, Böning gave it a new long-stroke crankshaft with plain instead of roller bearings. He replaced the side-valves by pushrod-operated overhead valves, and substituted a water pump for the thermo-syphon cooling system. The 20bhp put out by this engine gave the new car its name - the BMW 3/20.

Bodies were initially built at the Daimler-

Benz body plant in Sindelfingen, although the contract was later switched to Ambi-Budd in Berlin. They were some 3 inches lower than the old 3/15 types, though still very upright in appearance.

The 3/20 was replaced in February 1934 by the 309. Despite the introduction the year before of the six-cylinder 303, BMW still believed it could sell a four-cylinder car. So it took the 303 chassis and its stylish range of bodies and fitted it with a new 845cc engine. The assessment of the market was spot-on: between 1934 and 1936, the four-cylinder 309 sold three times as well as the six-cylinder 303.

The 309's engine was simply a four-cylinder version of the 303's six, which made use of the extra metal between the cylinders by having a larger 58mm bore. The 80mm stroke remained unchanged, however. With 22bhp, a typical 309 was capable of 50mph flat-out.

No kidney grille yet: a 1934 3/20 AM-4

Driving Machines

The six-cylinder cars: 303, 315 and 319

Many people regard the 303 as the first real BMW, and it certainly was the first BMW to have the now-famous 'kidney' grille, probably drawn up by body designer Peter Schimanowski.

The 303 was the cause of Max Friz's departure from BMW. He had designed an advanced aluminium-alloy four-cylinder engine to meet Franz Josef Popp's demand for more power. However, engine man Rudolf Schleicher proposed a small six-cylinder engine derived from the 3/20's four-cylinder: add two more cylinders, ran his argument, and you can machine it on the same tooling as the existing engine and so save money. Popp wasn't sure what to do, so he asked Wilhelm Kissel if he could consult the Daimler-Benz engineers! They voted for the six - and Friz left shortly afterwards.

The 303's 1173cc six-cylinder engine had the same overhead-valve layout as the 3/20's four, and the same bore and stroke dimensions. However, its block had been redesigned to give more metal between the bores and thus to allow for later capacity increases as well as wider main bearings. The chassis had the tubular side-members pioneered on the 3/20, but it had an improved front suspension, still with a transverse leaf spring but now with triangular lower control arms. The over-stiff rear suspension was the car's biggest weakness.

The fact that BMW's next six-cylinder car had a type designation so similar to the 3/15 applied to the licence-built Austin Seven often causes confusion. However, this time, the '15' didn't stand for the brake horsepower but rather the cubic capacity of nearly 1500cc - actually 1490cc.

The 315 was announced in April 1934. Its engine was a long-stroke version of the 303's small six, this time giving 34bhp and a top speed of about 60mph. Bodies, however, were almost identical to the 303's.

When Germany removed the tax penalties on large engines in 1935, BMW was quick to respond with a further enlarged six-cylinder, this time with 1911cc. First seen in the Roadster model (then called a 319/1), it was then offered with other bodies in the 319s which ran alongside the 315s between 1935 and 1937.

This 1934 303 saloon displays the new and distinctive BMW grille

The BMW Story

The Frazer-Nash connection

During the Austrian Alpine trials in 1933, H.J. Aldington of the British company Frazer-Nash saw the new six-cylinder BMWs in action. Deeply impressed, he sought the import franchise for UK market, only to find his main rival was none other than Sir Herbert Austin! This was some indication of how far BMW had come in just a few years: once licence-builders of Austin products, it was now in a position to licence its own products back to the British company.

However, BMW favoured the Frazer-Nash bid, and during 1935 the Frazer-Nash factory at Isleworth in Middlesex began assembly of right-hand drive 319s. With these Frazer-Nash-BMWs began a connection between the two companies which would last for more than 20 years.

Two-tone paint, a sloping tail, and smart rear wheel spats distinguished the 315/1 Roadster

Driving Machines

The Roadsters: 315/1 and 319/1

The greater performance of the bigger six-cylinder engines, the gradually recovering car market in Germany, and the need to improve the company's image were all factors in the development of the BMW Roadsters of the mid-1930s. These cars had strikingly attractive two-seater bodies designed by Peter Schimanowski. Their lines owed more than a little to the vogue for streamlined shapes, and also hinted at the way BMW styling would go over the next few years.

The Roadster was first shown with the 1490cc engine as a 315/1 at the Berlin Motor Show early in 1935. However, the engine was not the same as in regular 315s; it had three carburettors and 40bhp instead of the standard 34bhp, which powered the very much lighter car to a remarkable 74mph.

The similarly-bodied 319/1 followed, and was the first BMW to have the 1911cc engine. This, too, had three carburettors, and offered 55bhp compared to the 45bhp of the standard 319 engine. Top speed was 81mph.

This preserved 315/1 Roadster has the new grille and exposed wire wheels

The BMW Story

A THREE-WHEELER BMW

With car sales slipping in the early 1930s, the Eisenach car plant needed something to keep itself occupied. BMW's designers came up with a stop-gap product in the shape of a three-wheeler delivery cart of the type which Borgward and others had popularised in Germany during the tough economic climate of the 1920s.

The first examples had a 6bhp single-cylinder motorcycle engine of 200cc, and later ones a 12bhp 400cc single-cylinder. But the BMW three-wheeler lasted only a year in production. After Hitler's rise to power in 1933, Germany began to regain its pride and its confidence, and the cheap three-wheeler delivery cart quickly became a symbol of the bad old days. BMW saw the writing on the wall and stopped production after making just 600 examples.

THE AERO ENGINES

At the beginning of this period, BMW's aero engines consisted of its own Type VI V12 plus the Pratt and Whitney Hornet, built under licence from the American company. The Hornet was developed into the BMW 132, which shared its nine-cylinder air-cooled radial design and was about 5% more powerful.

As Germany began to re-arm, so the Luftwaffe placed big orders for the BMW engines. In 1935, the Munich aero engine plant was supplemented by a new one alongside the car factory at Eisenach, and in 1936 the German Air Ministry took the extraordinary step of granting BMW exclusive rights to build air-cooled radial aero engines in Germany.

Driving Machines

3/20   **1932-1934**   782cc four-cylinder with 20bhp
84.6-inch wheelbase, tubular chassis

7215 built   Independent front and rear suspension by transverse leaf springs
Bodies: two-door saloon, two-seater and four-seater convertible saloons, convertible, delivery van

303   **1933-1936**   1173cc six-cylinder with 30bhp
94.5-inch wheelbase, tubular chassis

2300 built   Independent front suspension, rear axle with semi-elliptic springs
Bodies: two-door saloon, two-door saloon with folding roof, convertible, sports convertible

309   **1934-1936**   845cc four-cylinder with 22bhp
94.5-inch wheelbase, tubular chassis

6000 built   Independent front suspension, rear axle with semi-elliptic springs
Bodies: two-door saloon, two-door saloon with folding roof, two-door tourer, convertible, sports convertible

315   **1934-1937**   1490cc six-cylinder with 34bhp
94.5-inch wheelbase, tubular chassis

9523 built   Independent front suspension, rear axle with semi-elliptic springs
Bodies: two-door saloon, two-door saloon with folding roof, two-door tourer, convertible, sports convertible

315/1   **1934-1936**   1490cc six-cylinder with 40bhp
94.5-inch wheelbase, tubular chassis

242 built   Independent front suspension, rear axle with semi-elliptic springs
Body: roadster

319   **1935-1937**   1911cc six-cylinder with 45bhp
94.5-inch wheelbase, tubular chassis

6544 built   Independent front suspension, rear axle with semi-elliptic springs
Bodies: two-door saloon, two-door saloon with folding roof, two-door tourer, convertible, sports convertible

319/1   **1934-1936**   1911cc six-cylinder with 55bhp
94.5-inch wheelbase, tubular chassis

102 built   Independent front suspension, rear axle with semi-elliptic springs
Body: roadster

The BMW Museum's own 328 Roadster is seen in this overhead shot.
The flashers on the front wings are a modern addition

Driving Machines

Chapter 3
INTERNATIONAL ACCLAIM, 1936-1941

By the mid-1930s, BMW had reached the limit of its production capacity. The new aero engine factory, opened in 1935 to cope with increasing orders, consumed a great deal of capital, and Chairman Franz Josef Popp was disinclined to spend more money to increase car production.

cars were unrecognisable as the descendants of the little Dixi first built a dozen years earlier.

The cornerstone of the BMW range in the later 1930s was the 326 saloon, announced at the Berlin Motor Show in February 1936

The 326: BMW's first four-door model and the first of a new generation of cars

Instead, he decided to boost profits by making more money on each car sold. BMW would therefore have to build grander cars, selling at higher prices which allowed room for higher profits as well. And so the company moved gradually further up-market in the later 1930s. From 1936, all BMWs had six-cylinder engines, and by the time production was halted by the War in 1941, the

and on sale that summer. In the five years of its production from 1936 to 1941, it outsold all the other BMW cars of the time put together. Combining boldly attractive styling with advanced mechanical elements, the 326 was a startlingly powerful statement of the abilities of a company which had been in the second rank of Germany's car makers.

Cabriolet versions of the 326 were also available.
The distinctive grille was now taller and slimmer

The BMW Story

The 326 was later joined by the 327 grand tourers and the 328 sports roadster - and BMW also developed other derivatives. All these cars had versions of the company's classic 2-litre six-cylinder engine. Based on the older 1911cc overhead-valve 'six', this was bored out to 1,971cc and proved smooth, powerful and tuneable - ideal for BMW's needs. Meanwhile, the aero

At the heart of almost every BMW built after 1936 was the magnificent 2-litre OHV 'six'. This example was for the 325 military vehicle

One of the most beautiful BMWs of all time: the 327 coupe. This example sports the rear wheel spats found on some cars and has two-toning typical of the period. Note how the headlamps were faired-in to the front wings

Driving Machines

Het snelste Motorrijwiel der wereld

Motor cycles continued to play an important part in BMW's success. This late-1930s racing machine has the familiar twin-cylinder, shaft-driven layout

met welke Ernst Henne op **28 November 1937** het absolute wereldrecord op **279,5 km/u** vestigde, alsmede de compressormachine die op **16 Juni 1939** de zwaarste der internationale wedstrijden, de Engelsche Tourist Trophy won, zijn het gevolg van grondige Duitsche onderzoekingsarbeid en technische wetenschap, die hun waardeering door de groote aanvraag naar **BMW**-motorrijwielen in alle deelen der wereld vonden. Deze successen brengen voor ons verplichtingen mede.

Wij rusten niet met ons werk; de waardevolle ervaringen in dezen oorlogstijd opgedaan worden door ons bewaard en zullen na den oorlog Europa ten goede komen.

BMW motor cycles set records, too. Ernst Henne rode this streamlined machine into the record books in 1937

engine and motor cycle divisions continued to bring in big profits. As the only authorised German producer of air-cooled radial aero engines after 1936, BMW was in demand both by military and civil aviation users. The motor cycles continued to sell well both at home and abroad, spearheaded by the successes of the works competition team. These were indeed heady days for BMW.

The BMW Story

Cornerstone - the 326

Chief designer Alfred Böning and Fritz Fiedler started work on the 326 late in 1934, designing for it a rigid platform-type chassis with box-section elements. They redesigned the existing BMW front suspension, mounting its transverse leaf-spring above instead of below the frame, and put torsion bar springs on the rear axle. Four-wheel hydraulic brakes became standard for the first time on a BMW, and the steering was by rack and pinion.

The 326 was BMW's first four-door saloon, and Peter Schimanowski's styling gave it a remarkably modern appearance. Its most striking feature was the front end, with enveloping wings and a grille which blended smoothly into the front panel. This grille, derived from earlier BMW designs, is the true ancestor of today's famous twin-kidney grille.

Panic stations - the 329

The 326's new styling immediately made existing production BMWs look old-fashioned. Afraid that sales of its roadsters - essentially fashionable cars - might therefore collapse while the 328 roadster was readied for production, BMW created a stop-gap model.

BMW grafted the 326's new front end onto the body of the 319/1, and called the result a 329. The car remained in production for just one year, bridging the gap between the 1936 arrival of the 326 and the launch of the new 328 in 1937.

Mix and match - the 320 and 321

The four-door 326 took BMW into new territory, but many of the company's customers still wanted a cheaper two-door saloon. So BMW developed the 320 to suit them.

The 320 was announced a year after the 326. It had a shortened 326 chassis and benefited from the latest BMW family styling. However, front and rear suspension were from the old 319, and the engine was detuned. A two-door cabriolet body was also made available.

The 320 lasted until 1938, and was replaced the following year by the 321. Essentially the same car, the 321 nevertheless had the improved 326-type front suspension and a restyled rear end derived from the big 335 model. There was also a third body-style in the shape of a sports cabriolet.

The 321 was never made in large quantities, mainly because the German war effort restricted materials supplies soon after its introduction. Production stopped in 1941.

The all-conquering 328

The 328 completely dominated sports car racing in Europe during the late 1930s, and played a major part in establishing BMW's reputation outside Germany.

The 315/1 and 319/1 roadsters had established a formidable sporting reputation for BMW in the mid-1930s, and it was automatic that they would be replaced by a new car related to the 326. Böning and Fiedler were given very little time to do the job, however, and drafted in Alex von Falkenhausen and Ernst Loof to help. Both would have major parts to play later in the BMW story.

A prototype 328 was ready for the Eifelrennen event in spring 1936, where it won its class. Private buyers had to wait until February 1937 to get their hands on one, however.

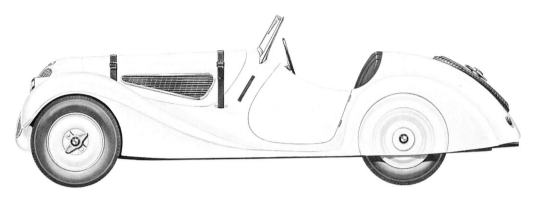

A classic almost from the moment it was announced, the BMW 328 roadster still looks good today. The rear spats were generally removed for competition work

The 328 kept the 94.5-inch wheelbase of the cars it replaced, and retained broadly similar styling. Structurally and mechanically, it was a compromise, with a tubular chassis frame, the front and rear suspension of the 319/1, and the 326's brakes. However, the real advance came in its engine.

This had the 2-litre block of the 326, but its redesigned cylinder head incorporated hemispherical combustion chambers. Relocated valves were operated by an ingenious cross-pushrod system, and double valve springs allowed higher revs. Three Solex carburettors completed the

The 328's triple-carburettor 2-litre engine

The so-called 'Mille Miglia' 328 of 1940 was bodied by Touring in Italy

The BMW Story

Different styling is in evidence on this Mille Miglia 328

picture. In production trim, the engine gave 80bhp, good for an astonishing 93mph. However, by 1940 the highly-tuned 328s used by the works teams were giving 120bhp.

Among the most famous 328s are the special 'streamliners' which ran in the factory team in 1939 and 1940. Inspired by the coachbuilder Wendler's 1938 streamlined coupé built for a private customer, BMW asked Carrozzeria Touring of Milan to make a closed coupé body for one of the works 328s in the 1939 Le Mans 24-hour race. The car took first in its class and fifth place overall, convincingly beating two standard-bodied works cars.

Plans to run a team of streamliners in the 1940 events were thwarted when Hitler's invasion of Poland in September 1939 ended international motorsport in Europe. Nevertheless, the streamlined 328s did run competitively in 1940 - in the Brescia Grand Prix, an event which pitted the best racers from Mussolini's Italy against those from their allies in Hitler's Germany. BMW entered four streamlined open 328s and a fastback coupé with bodywork designed by aerodynamicist Dr Wunibald Kamm which actually won the race. The Brescia event is sometimes called the 1940 Mille Miglia, and the cars therefore the Mille Miglia 328s.

Driving Machines

Glorious style - the 327

The 328 roadster did much for BMW's reputation outside Germany, but the real stars of the late-1930s range were the 327 coupés and cabriolets. Stunningly styled by Peter Schimanowski, they epitomise the German touring car of the period with their sleek yet curvaceous lines, their long bonnets, and the hint in their rear quarters of a wild animal about to pounce. Gorgeous two-toning and the option of rear wheel spats only enhance what are still among the most attractive cars ever to wear the BMW roundel.

The launch of the 327 followed that of the 326 saloon at a discreet distance: the cabriolet was announced in November 1937 and the coupé, in October the following year. Both had the short version of the 326's chassis as seen in the 320, but both also had the newer 326-type of front suspension allied to a rear end sprung on semi-elliptics. The short wheelbase and long-bonnet styling made seating strictly two-plus-two.

At first, the 327s came only with a high-compression version of the 326's engine. Then from April 1938, the triple-carburettor 328 engine was offered optionally, cars so equipped being rather clumsily described as 327/28 models. Production of all types stopped in 1941.

Frazer-Nash imported examples of the 327 into Britain, adding its own name to the BMW badge

Brescia, 1940: the single coupe version of the 328.

The BMW Story

Luxury class - the 335

Germany's abolition of tax penalties on larger-engined cars in 1935 led to the creation of the 2-litre 'six', and it also prompted BMW to develop a larger engine. This 3485cc six-cylinder was not a derivative of the 2-litre, although the two engines shared certain design features. It was announced initially in understressed 90bhp tune, but could certainly have been developed to give much more.

The model for which the big 'six' was developed was called the 335. A much larger car than the 2-litres of the mid-1930s, it was intended to compete against models from Horch, Wanderer and Mercedes-Benz. The 335 shared its styling with the 2-litre models, although it had a longer wheelbase, a wider track and a bigger boot. Its chassis and suspension followed 326 principles.

The prototype 335s were ready in 1938, but production was delayed until 1939 because of materials shortages caused by the German military build-up. The basic body was a four-door saloon, although 118 two-door cabriolets were built by Authenrieth of Darmstadt and 40 four-door cabriolets by Graber in Switzerland. Production was halted in 1941, after just 410 (or 462 - the figure is disputed) chassis had been built. Some remained unbodied.

A military BMW

As Hitler's Germany re-armed during the 1930s, so manufacturers were instructed to devote resources to military machinery. During 1936, the German Army designed an open cross-country car with four-wheel drive, and to build it they enlisted truck manufacturers Stoewer. A year later, Hanomag and BMW also began building examples. Nearly 13,000 of these vehicles were built between 1936 and 1943, the lion's share being made by Stoewer. BMW built just 3,259 between 1937 and 1940, all at its Eisenach car plant.

At BMW, the cross-country car was known as a model 325, but it never wore BMW badging and was never considered a proper BMW product. To simplify manufacture, however, the German Army had arranged for each of the vehicle's three manufacturers to install engines which they already had in production for civilian vehicles. The BMW-built examples therefore did have a BMW engine - the 326's 2-litre 'six'.

BRIEF SPECIFICATIONS

Note: For convenience, the BMW models of this period are listed in numerical order rather than in the order of their introduction.

320 **1937-1938** 1971cc six-cylinder with 45bhp
108.3-inch wheelbase, box-section platform chassis
4185 built Independent front suspension, rear axle with semi-elliptic
springs
Bodies: two-door saloon or two-door cabriolet

321 **1939-1941** 1971cc six-cylinder with 45bhp
108.3-inch wheelbase, box-section platform chassis
3692 built Independent front suspension, rear axle with semi-elliptic
springs
Body: two-door saloon, two-door cabriolet or two-door
sports cabriolet

326 **1936-1941** 1971cc six-cylinder with 50bhp
113-inch wheelbase, box-section platform chassis
15,936 built Independent front suspension, rear axle with torsion-bar
springs
Bodies: four-door saloon, two-door and four-door cabriolets

327 **1937-1941** 1971cc six-cylinder with 55bhp
108.3-inch wheelbase, box-section platform chassis
1304 built Independent front suspension, rear axle with semi-elliptic
springs
Body: two-door cabriolet (1937-1941) or two-door coupé
(1938-1941)

327/28 1938-1941 1971cc six-cylinder with 80bhp
108.3-inch wheelbase, box-section platform chassis
569 built Independent front suspension, rear axle with semi-elliptic
springs
Body: two-door cabriolet or two-door coupé

328 **1937-1939** 1971cc six-cylinder with 80bhp
94.5-inch wheelbase, tubular ladder-frame chassis
462 built Independent front suspension, rear axle with semi-elliptic
springs
Body: roadster

329 **1936-1937** 1911cc six-cylinder with 45bhp
94.5-inch wheelbase, tubular chassis
1179 built Independent front suspension, rear axle with semi-elliptic
springs
Bodies: cabriolet or sports cabriolet

335 **1939-1941** 3485cc six-cylinder with 90bhp
117.5-inch wheelbase, box-section platform chassis
410 built Independent front suspension, rear axle with torsion-bar
springs
Body: four-door saloon, four-door cabriolet or two-door
cabriolet

The BMW Story

The R-75 motor cycle combination was designed for military use

*Dating from 1943, this is a demonstration
cutaway BMW Type 109-003 jet aero engine*

Driving Machines

Chapter 4
WAR AND ITS AFTERMATH

Car production at BMW's Eisenach plant was halted in 1941, but the company remained busy. The German Armed Forces needed motor cycles in huge quantities, taking examples of the R12 until 1941 and then ordering huge quantities of the purpose-built R-75 sidecar combination. Aero engines were of course also in great demand for the Luftwaffe, and BMW remained in the forefront of development as well as building large quantities of extremely reliable engines. The 1939 purchase of Bramo, the Brandenburger Motorenwerke aero engine company based at Spandau, near Berlin, effectively doubled the company's production capacity and made BMW a vital element in the German war effort.

These, however, were just the company's better-known wartime activities. As explained in the previous chapter, the Eisenach car plant built a version of the Stoewer four-wheel drive staff car under the 325 name between 1937 and 1940. And after 1942, BMW also turned out quantities of stationary engines (both for military and civilian use) based on its pre-war car engines.

It was therefore hardly surprising that the Allies should have seized every available opportunity to bomb the BMW factories, and by the end of the war in 1945 the company's plants had been pounded to rubble. This itself would have been a major setback; but there was worse for BMW. The partitioning of Germany after the war left the Munich plants in the American-controlled zone while the Eisenach car plant fell to the Soviet Union. It soon became clear that the Soviets had no intention of encouraging links between their sector and the others, and that Eisenach was totally lost to BMW.

Even in Munich, things were not easy. Over the next couple of years, the Allied Control Commission removed all machinery which was of any use in the name of war reparations. BMW was forbidden to restart production of aero engines or cars, and what was left of the company was reduced to scratching a living from the manufacture of domestic necessities such as pots and pans. It also built a few bicycles - again, much in demand in a country where mechanised transport was out of the question for most people.

The 325 was a 4x4 military vehicle built by BMW and others; BMW's version had the company's 2-litre 'six'

The BMW Story

Intended to replace the 326, the 332 seen here in prototype form never entered production

None of this had crushed the BMW spirit, however. Technical chief Kurt Donath had rehired former chief designer Alfred Böning as early as 1945 and had set him to work designing a small-capacity motor cycle. One of a pair of pre-war car prototypes (known as the 332 and originally conceived as a 326 successor) was salvaged from the ruins in Munich and for a time was expected to enter production as soon as BMW was given permission to make cars again.

Meanwhile, the BMW expertise was in demand outside Germany. H.J. Aldington of Frazer-Nash (who had been BMW's British agents in the 1930s) attempted to bring most of the key BMW people to Britain in 1946, where he hoped they could resume their design activities. However, the British Government refused to grant work permits, and in the end only engine designer Fritz Fiedler came over. He was obliged to spend some time in jail as a 'war criminal' before being released to work in Britain - in fact, for Bristol, as one result of a complicated deal which Aldington had made.

As the chances of BMW ever rising from the ruins seemed remote in 1946, other key people left the company to seek their fortunes alone. Ernst Loof, former manag-er of the works racing team, gathered some colleagues around him and left to establish the Veritas company and build sports-racing cars. Engine designer Alex von Falkenhausen left to build sports-racing cars to which he gave the name of AFM. Neither company prospered, however, and both Loof and von Falkenhausen rejoined BMW in the 1950s.

As the BMW people dispersed, so the influence of the pre-war 328 model spread with them. The Bristol and Frazer-Nash in Britain, and the Veritas and AFM in Germany, all depended to a greater or lesser extent on the engineering which had made the 328 great. Meanwhile, in Soviet-occupied East Germany, BMW engineering once again came to the fore when the company's old Eisenach plant started building 321s and 327s - still bearing BMW badges despite the East German state control of the factory!

By 1948, things were becoming a little easier in West Germany, although living conditions were still grim for a large proportion of the populace. BMW was granted permission to build motorcycles again, and started by assembling what were effectively pre-war models from stocks of parts brought in from its dealers. Real manufacture was out of the question for the moment, because the company had no machine tools and no capital to buy them. However, Kurt Donath saw a way around this. He put the company into receivership,

Driving Machines

in the hope that it would be bought by someone who would invest in its future. And that was exactly what happened; BMW was bought by two bankers from Munich, and before long the new machine tools which the company so desperately needed arrived at the Milbertshofen plant.

Production of the R-24 motorcycle started during 1948, and was followed by that of a smaller, short-lived model. Demand was such that the company quickly got back on its feet. Within five years, 100,000 motor cycles had been made - a figure which had taken the 15 years from 1923 to 1938 to equal in the more auspicious days before the war. BMW had been pulled back from the brink, and now it was time to start considering a return to car production.

Who ran the company?

When the war broke out in 1939, BMW's head was still Franz Josef Popp, the industrial tycoon who had built the company up since 1917. But Popp retired in October 1942, and a new Board took over. Among its members were Fritz Fiedler as technical director, and Kurt Donath, who rapidly became the driving force behind BMW.

After Donath put the company into receivership in 1948, it was rescued by the bankers Hans-Karl von Mangoldt-Reiboldt (who became BMW's President) and Hanns Grewenig (who became the Sales Director).

The motor cycles

BMW built four major types of motor cycle during the 1940s, the R-12, the R-35, the R-75 and the R-24. In addition, there was a short-lived two-stoke machine built during 1948 called the R-10.

The R-12 was introduced in 1935 and lasted until 1941. It had the familiar BMW

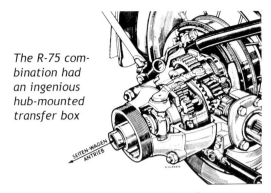

The R-75 combination had an ingenious hub-mounted transfer box

characteristics of an air-cooled flat-twin engine and shaft drive to the rear wheels. This 746cc machine was matched by the similar but smaller R-35, which had a 340cc single-cylinder engine. Both saw military service during the war.

Familiar from war movies will be the R-75, which was actually designed by the Army. It was a motor-cycle and sidecar combination, in which the sidecar's wheel was driven by a shaft from the rear wheel of the bike. The German Army used it for a variety of purposes, including light towing duties. The basic design was shared with Zündapp, whose version used that company's own engine. The R-75 had the 746cc BMW air-cooled twin. A total of 16,510 were built between 1940 and 1944.

The post-war R-24 was a 250cc single-cylinder machine, as usual with shaft drive to the rear wheel. Ready by July 1947, it did not enter production until 1948. Its companion 125cc two-stroke model ceased production after less than a year when BMW agreed with Auto Union not to build

BMW's first post-war motor cycle was the 1948 R-24

The BMW Story

two-stroke motor-cycles; in return, Auto Union agreed that its DKW marque would not build four-stroke cars.

The aero engines

Since 1936, BMW had been the only German company permitted by the Air Ministry to build air-cooled radial engines, and the company's Eisenach and Munich factories had been kept busy supplying both military and civilian customers. New designs were under way before the war broke out - and one in particular demonstrated BMW's technical leadership in the field - but the company badly needed the input of new ideas which came from its 1939 acquisition of the Bramo aero engine company.

One of BMW's most successful wartime engines was introduced in 1939. This was the Type 801, a 14-cylinder twin-bank radial engine which saw service in early versions of the Focke-Wulf 190 fighter. The engine was built in a new plant which BMW erected at Allach for the purpose. By 1945, BMW had developed the original 2000bhp design to give 2400bhp, and to give 1800bhp at 37,000 feet when fitted with a turbocharger.

However, radial piston engines were not new to BMW. Much more exciting was the company's pioneering work on the gas turbine or jet aero engine. Development of the revolutionary powerplant first sketched up in 1938 was nevertheless slow, and the jet-powered Messerschmitt Me262 fighter did not fly until 1942. The Type 109-003 engine which powered it was later abandoned, but BMW was working on a much bigger engine called the 109-018 when the war ended. This remarkable design was suitable for use as either a turbo-jet or a turboprop engine, and would have developed around 7000bhp in production trim.

Bristol and Frazer-Nash - the 'British BMWs'

In Britain, Frazer-Nash had been importing BMWs since 1935, enjoying an extremely close relationship with the company. So it was perhaps not entirely unexpected when the company's H.J. Aldington presented himself in Munich after the war had ended and suggested that BMW's key people might like to come and join him in Britain. But for the intervention of the British Government, it might well have happened.

Instead, only engine designer Fritz Fiedler came to Britain, and in 1948 he designed the new High Speed sports car for Frazer-Nash, using what was effectively a modified 328 chassis and the Bristol-built derivative of the 328's 2-litre engine. An early example came third in the 1949 Le Mans, and all subsequent models were known as Le Mans Replicas.

The Bristol connection was again H.J. Aldington's work. Faced with a large factory which was no longer needed for aircraft manufacture after the war, the Bristol Aeroplane Company decided to use it to build cars. Aldington sold his BMW manufacturing licence to Bristol, and as part of the deal secured the right to buy Bristol-built engines at preferential rates for his own cars. Fritz Fiedler went to Bristol to help the company get started as another part of that deal, only coming to Frazer-Nash later on.

Bristol never denied the close relationship of its first car to the pre-war BMWs. Even its name - 400 - was chosen to show that it was a development of the '300-series' BMWs of the 1930s. Its engine was a direct copy of the 328's 2-litre type, and its bodywork a rather ungainly adaptation of the 327 coupé. Even the twin-nostril grille was carried over intact.

Driving Machines

The British certainly didn't improve the styling of the pre-war BMW 327 when they borrowed it for the Bristol 400 in 1947

The 328-derived engine remained in production at Bristol until 1961, by which time it had been enlarged to 2.2 litres and was pumping out 160bhp. Bristol-powered sports racers dominated the 2-litre class in the 1950s in Britain, and the engine was acknowledged as one of the finest competition powerplants of its day.

The East German BMW

When BMW's Eisenach factory fell into Soviet hands at the end of the war, it quickly became part of the large Autovelo combine. Body dies and welding equipment were stripped from the Ambi-Budd plant in Berlin to be taken to Eisenach, and by the end of 1945 the factory was ready to start production of the pre-war 321 saloon. In 1948, modified versions of the 327 coupes and cabriolets also went into production, and from 1949 a modified 326 became available under the 340 name.

All these cars carried the blue and white BMW badge, much to the annoyance of the parent company in Munich. So in September 1949, BMW legally divorced itself from its former Eisenach plant. The cars remained in production, however, with the blue and white roundel changed to a red and white one, and the name changed from BMW to EMW (Eisenach Motoren Werke)! The last one was built in 1945, when the factory switched to a new type of car, based on a pre-war DKW prototype and badged as a Wartburg. That name came from a 1930 roadster derivative of the BMW 3/15!

AFM and Veritas

The technology of the 328 lived on in West Germany, too - in two small-volume marques set up by former BMW employees. Alex von Falkenhausen established AFM in 1946 (the initials were from his name, plus M for Munich) to build sports and racing cars, initially using an 1100cc MG engine but later graduating to a six-cylinder based heavily on the 2-litre from the 328. Later on, he attempted to enter the touring-car market with sports coupes and cabriolets using a six-cylinder Opel engine, but the venture folded, by 1954 von Falkenhausen was back with BMW - as its chief of engine development.

Ernst Loof founded Veritas in 1947, initially to build single-seater racers. These were fitted with second-hand 328 engines and established a name for the company. Loof also wanted to build road cars, and for these he designed a 1,988cc development of the 328 engine which went into production in 1950. The castings were made by Heinkel - another former German aircraft maker then looking for business. None of the road cars sold very well; and nor did the Dyna-Veritas, a two-seater convertible using running gear from the Dyna-Panhard. (The Veritas factory was in the French occupied zone of Germany, and Loof had correctly guessed that he would get financial support from the occupying authorities if he built a car around French components!). The last Veritas was built in 1953; Loof returned to BMW and joined its styling and body engineering division.

The BMW Story

Autenrieth built the bodies for the distinctive and prestigious 502 coupes. Styling resembled the saloons, but note particularly the position of the headlamps

The little 331 prototype of 1950 looked like a shrunken 501! Its concept was inspired by the pre-war Fiat 500

Driving Machines

Chapter 5
BACK IN ACTION

BMW entered the 1950s with its motor cycle division up and running once more but with its car division still dormant and its aero engine business still banned by the Allied Control Commission. Yet the company which had been completely broken by 1945 made a truly remarkable recovery.

Company chief Kurt Donath recognised that the biggest problem facing the car division was its lack of tooling, all confiscated during the mid-1940s in the name of war reparations. So, once BMW had started on the road to recovery in 1948 with its resumption of motor cycle production, he began to look for new business which would bring tooling with it.

First, he approached Ford in the USA and suggested that BMW might build the US giant's trucks under licence for the German market; but that proposal failed because Ford had its own plans to build trucks in Germany. Then he tried Simca in France, offering to buy the manufacturing rights and the tooling for the Simca 8, a licence-built Fiat which the firm was soon to replace with a new car of its own design. That approach failed because Simca wanted to retain the tooling.

BMW's voluntary receivership late in 1948 brought in the financial support which

Donath had hoped it would when the company was bought by two bankers. It was probably this which prompted the start of work on a new car, an economy model called the 331 which would probably have sold quite well in the difficult economic climate of the times. But Sales Director Hanns Grewenig vetoed the plan after a prototype had been built, arguing that the company did not yet have the resources to build a high-volume car. Instead, he insisted, BMW should build smaller numbers of more expensive machines, concentrating on high quality. It was a strategy which had saved Britain's Rover during the 1930s, but it would backfire on BMW in the 1950s.

Nevertheless, Grewenig persuaded the rest of the BMW Directors that the company needed to regain the up-market position it had enjoyed in the later 1930s. Design and development work therefore switched to a much bigger car, which logically took the name of 501. (The pre-war cars were 300-series models, Bristol's British derivative had claimed the 400 number, and so the 501 was number one in the 500 series which followed.)

However, the company was still in a perilous position. In May 1951, its capital stock was written down. The new car was announced at the Frankfurt Show some

A prototype 501 was at the 1951 Frankfurt Motor Show, but the car had been modified in detail by the time production began just over a year later

The BMW Story

four months later, but BMW had still not installed the new body plant needed to build it. As a result, production was seriously delayed; the first cars reached customers in October 1952, and the bodies of these were actually assembled by Karrosserie Baur in Stuttgart under contract to BMW. A total of 2045 cars were bodied by Baur - almost all the first two years' production - before BMW got its new body plant into operation at Milbertshofen.

At this stage, BMW was teetering on a knife-edge. Sales of the 501s were slow, and in 1954 the company introduced a new and cheaper entry-level model called the 501A to tempt customers. To pay off outstanding bank loans, the Allach engine plant had to be sold off to MAN in April 1955. Yet motor cycle sales were continuing to increase, and BMW seem to have hoped that profits from these would help the car division to expand. Then there was the prospect of further profits from a reactivated aero engine division, for which the Allied Control Commission gave its permission during 1955.

So BMW embarked upon a very rapid expansion of its car range, an expansion which with hindsight appears to have been too rapid. At the September 1955 Frankfurt Show, the company introduced a breathtaking array of new models.

The original six-cylinder 501, already complemented by a V8 version, was now joined by a third version with a larger-capacity V8; and that engine went into no fewer than three completely new models. These were the 503 grand tourers, the 505 limousine, and the 507 sports car. And on top of that, there was a new model right at the bottom of the range - a licence-built 'bubble car' originating in Italy. Though it must have gone against the grain, Grewenig had agreed to this econo-

my model when it had become obvious that the big 501 saloons were not bringing in the profits which BMW needed.

This calculated gamble went badly wrong. It was during 1955 that motor cycle sales began to slip, and by 1957 they had reached a post-war low. Aero engine production took some time to get under way again, and car sales slipped from 4567 in 1955 to just 1700 in 1957. The expected profits did not materialise, and the new models simply ended up complicating production and costing the company money. Early in 1957, both Kurt Donath and Hanns Grewenig retired from the Board, and it was only a huge loan from the Deutsche Bank in 1958 which saved BMW from going under once again. And over the next few years, Boardroom battles would see several changes of personnel at the top of BMW.

The baby BMW

BMW intended to make an economy car long before it acquired the rights to the Isetta bubble-car, and in the late 1940s work began on a baby BMW called the 331. However, the project was abandoned when sales director Hanns Grewenig decreed that BMW should aim higher up the market ladder.

There is no doubt that design chief Alfred Böning started by taking a long and careful look at the Fiat 500 - then still in its original 1930s Topolino form. He adapted the 600cc air-cooled flat-twin engine from the R-51 motor cycle to a four-speed gearbox, and gave the car a simple live rear axle. Peter Schimanowski designed the two-seater body which combined pre-war BMW styling cues with baby-Fiat dimensions.

It was not to be, but pictures of the 1950 331 prototype show clearly that this car's styling was the 'missing link' between the pre-war saloons and the Baroque Angels.

The Baroque Angels

Extra brightwork marked out the 502 of 1955-1958

The 500-series cars may not have been BMW's most glamorous products, but these big, sturdy middle-class machines were the mainstay of the company's car division from 1951 to 1964. They were nicknamed 'Barockengel' - Baroque Angels - because their bulbous and flowing lines reminded people of the carved wooden figures in south German and Austrian churches of the Baroque period (17th and early 18th centuries).

The first 501s had an updated version of the pre-war 2-litre six-cylinder engine. In 1954, this was supplemented by a 2.6-litre V8 with around 50% more power; the six-cylinder 501 was also uprated, and coupé and cabriolet bodies were announced.

The styling was dated by the time of this 2600 or 3200 from the early 1960s

In 1955, BMW announced the 502 range, basically the same cars with extra equipment. These had either an uprated 2.6-litre V8 or a new big-bore 3.2-litre V8. The 501 V8 remained unchanged, but the six-cylinder 501s were given an enlarged 2.1-litre engine. Then the 3.2-litre V8 was in turn uprated for 1957's 502 3.2-litre Super. In 1958, the 502 models were renamed as the BMW 2.6-litre, BMW 3.2-litre and the BMW 3.2 Super. All 501 V8 production ended, but the six-cylinder 501s remained available with their original names.

Heidemann built the ambulance body on this 502

Front disc brakes and the (formerly optional) servo became standard on the 3.2 Super in 1959 and on the ordinary 3.2 a year later. Then in 1961, the six-cylinder 501s ceased production. The 2.6-litre was renamed a 2600, given the servo and front discs, and joined by a 2600L with more power and better trim. The 3.2 became a 3200L and the 3.2 Super became a 3200 Super (also known as a 3200S). Its 160bhp V8 made it the fastest saloon then made in Germany and among the fastest in the world.

The last Baroque Angels were built in March 1964.

The BMW Story

The V8 engine

The pre-war 2-litre BMW engine was a remarkable piece of design, but the company knew it needed something more modern to go with the up-market image it wanted for its cars. So chief designer Alfred Böning started work on a new engine almost as soon as the 501 was settled for production.

That engine was a V8 - standard fare in the USA but almost unknown in Europe. Not surprisingly, Böning therefore turned to the USA for inspiration, and paid special attention to the very latest overhead-valve design from General Motors. This was the 303 cubic inch (4.9-litre) Oldsmobile Rocket V8.

Like the Oldsmobile engine, the BMW V8 had its cylinder banks set at 90 degrees to one another, with the cylinder bores slightly offset. It shared the American engine's five-bearing crankshaft and its duplex chain drive to a central camshaft, which operated the overhead valves through pushrods and rockers. But BMW went a stage further than GM; whereas the Americans were still wedded to all-iron construction, the Bavarians made both block and cylinder heads of light alloy, adding cast-iron wet liners to prevent premature bore wear. To suit European conditions, BMW's engine had just over half the capacity of the Oldsmobile, at 2.6 litres.

When Fritz Fiedler returned to BMW in 1952 as Research and Development Chief after his sojourn with Frazer-Nash in England, he took over work on the V8. Cash was tight, however,

and the engine's launch was delayed until the Geneva Motor Show of March 1954. The original 95bhp V8 was subsequently developed further, being bored out to give 3.2 litres in 1955 and going on to give as much as 160bhp by the time production ended in 1965.

This first BMW V8 was another remarkable engine - good enough for General Motors to take a close look when it came to develop its own small-block alloy V8 at the end of the 1950s. That 3.5-litre design was later sold to Rover, which has now been using derivatives of it for nearly 30 years! A comparison between BMW and Buick/Rover blocks reveals some startling similarities.

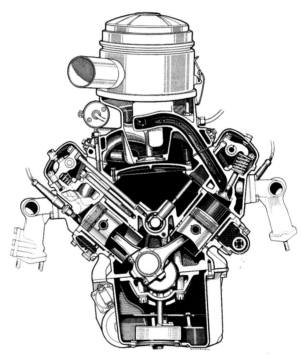

This cutaway of the 2.6-litre V8 engine shows the 90-degree vee of the cylinder banks, the central camshaft and the pushrod-operated overhead valve gear. If the layout was not new, the decision to make the engine of light alloy most certainly was

Driving Machines

Special Angels

The separate-chassis construction of the Baroque Angels made them an ideal basis for special bodywork. BMW itself catalogued a number of special bodies for the cars between 1954 and 1958, and a handful of others were built by coachbuilders to special order, both in this period and later. All these cars are rare.

Two-door coupé bodies were available on the 501A, 501/3 and 502 chassis. The majority were by Baur of Stuttgart, and had curvaceous lines adapted from those of the standard saloons. A few others with more angular lines were built by Autenrieth of Darmstadt.

Two-door cabriolet bodies were available on the same chassis as the coupés. Once again, Baur built examples with styling to match the saloons, while Autenrieth built a handful of more radically different cars.

The four-door cabriolet was a Baur body,

The Swiss coachbuilder Beutler built this two-door coupe on a V8-engined chassis in the late 1950s

and was in theory available only on the 1954 501A chassis. However, some examples also seem to have been fitted to later 502 chassis.

In Switzerland, Beutler of Thun built two (different) coupés, both on V8-engined chassis, and Ramseir of Worblaufen made a coupé on a 3.2-litre engined chassis in 1960. In Italy, Vignale of Turin built a single 3200 to a design by Michelotti.

Baur built the cabriolet body on this 502 V8 chassis dating from the late 1950s

The BMW Story

A BMW limousine - the 505

The 505 limousine was one of four completely new models announced to broaden the BMW range at the 1955 Frankfurt Show, and it was the only one of them not to enter production. In fact, just two examples were built. BMW historians today still debate the precise reasons, but it seems probable that the car was a victim of the company's deepening financial crisis.

The 505 sat on a long (119.5-inch) wheelbase version of the chassis used for the 501 and 502, and had the single-carb, 120bhp, version of the brand-new 3.2-litre V8 engine. The Frankfurt Show car had a body styled by Michelotti and built by Ghia-Aigle in Switzerland, and BMW planned to offer the 505 in chassis-only form, for bodying by specialist coachbuilders. This was Rolls-Royce territory: even Mercedes-Benz built its own bodies for the 505's natural rival, the big 300 limousine.

The Show car is now in BMW's museum.

An imposing failure: just two examples of the 505 limousine were built

Driving Machines

THE BAROQUE ANGELS

All models had a chassis consisting of box-section side members and tubular cross-members, with a wheelbase of 111.6 inches. In all cases torsion bar springs were used on all four wheels; the independent front suspension had twin wishbones and the live rear axle had additional location from an A-frame pivoting on the top of the differential casing.

First-generation six-cylinder   **Total built: 2125**

| 501 | 1952-1954 | 1971cc six-cylinder with 65bhp |
| | Bodies: | four-door saloon |

Second-generation six-cylinder   **Total built: 3327**

501A	1954-1955	1971cc six-cylinder with 72bhp
501B	1954-1955	1971cc six-cylinder with 72bhp
		(The 501B had plusher trim than the 501A but was otherwise identical)
	Bodies:	501A and 501B - four-door saloon; 501A for 1954 only - coupé or two-door and four-door cabriolets

Third-generation (2.1-litre) six-cylinder   **Total built: 3459**

| 501/3 | 1955-1958 | 2077cc six-cylinder with 72bhp |
| | Bodies: | four-door saloon, coupé or two-door cabriolet |

2.6-litre V8, base models   **Total built: 5914**

501 V8	1954-1958	2580cc V8 with 95bhp
2.6	1958-1961	2580cc V8 with 95bhp
2600	1961-1962	2580cc V8 with 100bhp
	Bodies:	4-door saloon

2.6-litre V8, luxury models   **Total built: 3117**

502	1954-1958	2580cc V8 with 100bhp
	Bodies:	four-door saloon, coupé or two-door and four-door cabriolets
2.6 Luxus	1958-1961	2580cc V8 with 100bhp
2600L	1961-1964	2580cc V8 with 110bhp
	Bodies:	four-door saloon

3.2-litre V8, base models   **Total built: 2537**

502 Super	1955-1958	3168cc V8 with 120bhp
3.2	1958-1961	3168cc V8 with 120bhp
3200L	1961-1962	3168cc V8 with 140bhp
	Bodies:	four-door saloon

3.2-litre V8, luxury models   **Total built: 1328**

3.2 Super	1957-1961	3168cc V8 with 140bhp
3200S	1961-1963	3168cc V8 with 160bhp
	Bodies:	four-door saloon

Total all models: 21,807

The BMW Story

Sublime...the 507 Roadster was intended to capture the US sports car market, but was never as successful as its makers had hoped

Ridiculous or not, the licence-built Isetta bubble-car helped to keep BMW going in the 1950s. The gulf between this and the 507 was immense

Driving Machines

Chapter 6
THE SUBLIME AND THE (FAINTLY) RIDICULOUS

The sturdy middle-class Baroque Angel saloons took BMW back into the car market in the early 1950s, but as the decade wore on they were joined by a variety of other models. In fact, the second half of the Fifties was a time of incredible contrasts at BMW - a time when the car ranges really did encompass both the sublime (in the shape of expensive exotica) and the faintly ridiculous (in the shape of bubble-cars). If only the company had also had something more than the Baroque Angels to plug the yawning gap in the middle ...

The Baroque Angels may have been respectable and well-engineered cars, but they were not big volume-sellers. It was the success of the motorcycle division which kept BMW afloat in the first half of the Fifties, and the company's management wisely planned to expand its car activities as early as possible. During the middle Fifties, it did this in two ways. The first was by trying to enter the vast American market with a pair of high-priced exotics, and the second was by trying to enter the mass-production market with cheap economy cars.

Sadly, the exotic 503 grand tourer and 507 roadster did not attract the sales the company hoped for, and BMW probably lost money on every one sold. And, as the German economy strengthened in the middle Fifties, buyers wanted cars which reflected their new-found wealth, and turned away from the economy models which carried with them a kind of stigma of poverty.

At the same time, and for similar reasons, the motorcycle market collapsed. From peak sales of almost 30,000 in 1954, motorcycle sales rapidly declined, to 23,000 in 1955 and to just 5400 in 1957. Car sales fell from their 1955 peak of 4567 to 3400 in 1956 and to an abysmal 1700 in 1957. The resumption of activity by the aero-engine division in 1956 went some way to offsetting these catastrophic losses, but there was no way out: the banks refused to lend the money BMW needed to develop a new mid-range car because the company's future looked so rocky. It was no coincidence that Chairman Kurt Donath and Sales Director Hanns Grewenig chose to resign in 1957.

BMW's new Chairman, Heinrich Richter-Brohm, managed to secure a loan from the Deutsche Bank in 1958, and with this he set in motion the development of the new 700 model. He also set the BMW engineers to work on the design of a new four-cylinder engine for an eventual mid-range car, but disgruntled shareholders were not prepared to wait, and he was forced out of office in 1959. In his stead came Dr Herbert Quandt, a financier who had bought up a large block of BMW shares. Quandt would stay at the helm of BMW for a very long time.

However, the turnaround had already begun. The 700, introduced in 1959, proved a real hit, and brought in the revenue which allowed BMW to devote more resources to the forthcoming mid-range car. That car, the 1500 or New Class saloon, arrived in 1961 and completely changed BMW's fortunes over the next few years.

Cheap motoring - the Isetta 250 and 300

BMW built the Isetta bubble-car under licence from Iso S.p.a. of Italy, who was primarily a maker of motor scooters and three-wheeler utilities. Iso introduced the Isetta in 1953, and also sold a licence for its production to Velam in France. Iso's owner, Count Renzo Rivolta, eventually spent the profits from these agreements on making the Euro-American Iso Rivolta and Iso Grifo supercars.

The BMW Story

Later versions of the Isetta had large side windows, like this export-model 300 with two-tone paintwork

The BMW Isetta 250 dispensed with Iso's two-stroke engine, using instead the four-stroke 247cc single-cylinder from the R25 motorcycle. From February 1956, there was a companion-model Isetta 300, with the more powerful 297cc engine from the R27 motorcycle. Other changes included smaller headlamp cowls after 1955 and a completely revised glass area with larger side windows from October 1956.

The original Iso car, the BMW version, and the Velam all had twin rear wheels, but a version of the Isetta 300 built under licence from BMW in Britain from 1958 actually had a single rear wheel, because three-wheelers attracted less Purchase Tax and their road fund licence was cheaper! Just 1750 three-wheelers were built.

In the mid-Fifties, the Isetta cost just 20% as much as the cheapest of the Baroque Angel 501 saloons.

Early Isettas were characterised by triangular side windows. Note also the long headlamp bodies

Driving Machines

The 600

The 600 was a logical progression from the
Isetta which must have seemed like a good
idea at the time, but sales of just over
34,000 in two years never really matched
BMW's expectations. Part of the problem
was the price - the 600 was only barely
cheaper than the entry-level VW Beetle.
But it was also undeniable that buyers in
the late Fifties wanted cars that looked
like cars, and were losing interest in economy models which suggested that their
owners might not have much money.
Without the short-lived vogue for economy
cars which followed the Suez crisis of
1956-1957, the 600 might have flopped
badly.

Designed by Willy Black, the 600 was
unashamedly intended as an enlarged
Isetta with more power and a 'proper'
four-wheel configuration. Its front end was
pretty much unchanged from the Isetta's,
but the wheelbase had been stretched to
accommodate four seats, and a conventional rear axle had been added. This
introduced to BMW the semi-trailing-arm
independent suspension which would be
seen on almost every new model for the
next four decades.

The extra size and weight demanded a
more powerful engine than the Isetta's,
and so the 600 had yet another motorcycle
powerplant - this time the 582cc twin from
the recently-defunct R67. Top speed was
64mph.

The 700

The 700 was really the car which pulled
BMW around in the late Fifties. Once again
it was an upward progression in size from
what had gone before - this time, the 600
chassis was stretched. But by the time it
entered production, the 700 had become
BMW's first unitary-construction car.
The 700 was again masterminded by Willy
Black, the man who had designed the 600
which it replaced. Black drew on the company's motorcycle technology once again,
although this time he enlarged the twin-
cylinder engine of the R67 motorcycle to
get the power he needed for this larger
car.

Styling was by the Italian Giovanni
Michelotti, and its themes certainly
echoed those of his Triumph Herald, an
exact contemporary of the 700. His first
sketch was for a slant-roof coupé, which
appealed to BMW although they wanted
more room in the passenger cabin.
Michelotti therefore sketched up a saloon
variant - never as pretty - and the
Bavarians decided to build them both. The
700 Coupé entered production in August

The BMW Story

Most attractive of the Michelotti-styled 700s was the cabriolet, built in Stuttgart by Baur

1959 and the 700 Saloon joined it at the end of the year.

Even though the 700 was more expensive than a VW Beetle, its chic Italian styling brought in the buyers. Over the six years of its production, the car sold more than 188,000 examples and became BMW's best-selling car since 1945.

Engine power increased over those six years, and from 1961 there was an upmarket Luxus version. Then in 1962, the 700 was renamed the BMW LS. Among the most desirable of these small cars is the Baur-built cabriolet, but the most exciting was the limited-production 700RS, a competition roadster of which just 19 were built between 1961 and 1963.

Exotica - the 503

The 503 was one way in which BMW hoped to crack the American market in the mid-Fifties. The Baroque Angel saloons were not going to sell well in the USA, but BMW thought that an elegant grand tourer with the saloon's running gear and powerful V8 engine might.

The 503 used the saloon's perimeter-frame chassis as well as its running gear, and it had an all-alloy body designed by Albrecht Goertz. Goertz was a German who had worked with the Raymond Loewy design studio on Studebakers in the late Forties and early Fifties, then became a naturalised American and set up his own design studio. He was persuaded to submit

There is something very Italian about the appearance of this 503 cabriolet, even though its styling was by Goertz

Driving Machines

The 503 came as a closed coupe as well, when it looked rather more substantial

designs for the 503 (and the 507) by BMW's American importer, Max Hoffmann. Tempted by Hoffmann's offer to take a Goertz-designed 503 in quantity, BMW embraced the Goertz proposals and showed a prototype at the 1955 Frankfurt Show. Production began the following May.

Sadly, the 503's styling was flawed. The long bonnet hinted at power, but was spoiled by an ugly snub nose incorporating the traditional BMW grille. Electric windows were advanced for the time, and the power-operated hood on cabriolets was a first for a German car. But the saloon gearbox, mounted between the seats and operated by a woolly column change, did the 503 no favours. After September 1957, the gearbox was mounted conventionally so that a floor change could be fitted.

The 503 was always an expensive and exclusive car, competing with such exotics as the (more costly) Mercedes-Benz 300SC and the Bentley Continental. Production averaged 100 or so a year, and it is likely that no two examples were exactly alike. Only a handful were delivered with right-hand drive. Despite their aesthetic short-comings, the cars are very much sought-after today.

Classic roadster - the 507

The 507 is probably the most widely-recognised classic BMW of the Fifties. Like its great rival the Mercedes-Benz 300SL, it was inspired by the US importer Max Hoffmann, who told BMW he could sell a high-performance sports car in large quantities if the company could deliver.

The BMW trademark grille was re-styled to suit the low nose of the 507

The BMW Story

In 1954, Ernst Loof (now back at BMW after the failure of his own Veritas company) designed and built a prototype on the 502 chassis with a 2.6-litre V8 engine. However, an alternative style put forward by Albrecht Goertz at Hoffmann's suggestion won the day. The Goertz style was for a curvaceous roadster with optional hard top. It was a shape which has worn incredibly well over the years, and examples of the 507 now change hands for very large sums of money.

The production cars had the 3.2-litre V8 in twin-carburettor form with 150bhp or, for the USA only, with 165bhp. Acceleration and top speed depended on which of the three optional axle ratios was chosen, but the performance of a 507 was broadly comparable with that of the contemporary XK140 Jaguar. BMW claimed a 507 was capable of 136mph with the tallest 3.42:1 gearing, although 120mph was probably nearer the truth.

Yet this remarkable machine was never a strong seller. One problem was cost; another was BMW's inability to get production under way. Despite a Frankfurt 1955 announcement, the first cars were not delivered until the next year. By then, the Mercedes had become too well-entrenched as the definitive supercar, and the 300SL gullwing coupé's mutation into a roadster model in 1957 removed the 507's most obvious advantage. Lack of boot space in the first cars was also a major failing, and BMW was forced to introduce a smaller 'optional' fuel tank to free up more room.

Just 254 507s were sold between 1956 and 1959, all with left-hand drive. Some of the very last had disc brakes at the front instead of the all-drum system.

BMW motorcycles in the Fifties

The decade divided neatly into two for BMW motorcycles, with the major changes to the range coming in 1955-1956. As the Fifties opened, the R24 single of 1948 gained plunger rear suspension to become an R25, and was joined by the revived pre-war R51 twin. Then in 1951, the range was swelled by the R67, with a more powerful 582cc OHV twin. Geneva 1952 saw the arrival of the R68 sports derivative of the R67, with a twin-leading-shoe front brake and genuine 100mph performance.

The changeover year was 1955, which brought new frames and forks for the R25 and R67, plus no fewer than three new models. These were the R26 (247cc single), the R50 (494cc twin) and the R69 (594cc twin). The R25 and R67 disappeared in 1956, when the 594cc R60 took over the bigger bike's role as a sidecar machine. The R60 also found favour with police and military users.

Competition successes kept BMW at the forefront of the two-wheel sector during the Fifties, and Wilhelm Noll's sidecar world championship in 1954 began a run of 20 years in which BMW dominated such events. The middle of the decade also saw BMW bikes set a number of world records, mainly for long-distance or long-duration events. Nevertheless, declining sales by the end of the Fifties reflected BMW's persistent reliance on refined, expensive machines at a time when cheaper bikes were sweeping the market.

BMW Isetta

model	period	engine type
Isetta 250	1955-1962	247cc single-cyl, with 12bhp
Isetta 300	1956-1962	298cc single-cyl, with 13bhp

Total built: **136,567**

BMW 600

model	period	engine type
600 saloon	1957-1959	582cc twin-cyl, with 19.5bhp

Total built: **34,318**

BMW 700 and LS

model	period	engine type
700 saloon	1959-1962	697cc twin-cyl, with 30bhp
700 Coupé	1959-1964	697cc twin-cyl, with 30bhp
700 Sport	1960-1963	697cc twin-cyl, with 40bhp
700CS Coupé	1963-1964	697cc twin-cyl, with 40bhp
700 Cabriolet	1961-1964	697cc twin-cyl, with 40bhp
LS Luxus	1962-1965	697cc twin-cyl with 30bhp (1962-1963) or 40bhp (from February 1963)
LS Coupé	1964-1965	697cc twin-cyl, with 40bhp

Total built: **188,121**

BMW 503

model	period	engine type
503 Coupé	1956-1960	3168cc V8-cyl, with 140bhp
503 Cabriolet	1956-1960	3168cc V8-cyl, with 140bhp

Note: some of the last cars had the 150bhp 507 engine

Total built: **412**

BMW 507

model	period	engine type
507	1956-1959	3168cc V8-cyl, with 150bhp or (USA only) 165bhp

Total built: **254**

The BMW Story

When BMW bought Glas in the mid-1960s, the company's stylish sports coupe was re-engined to become a BMW 1600GT

However, the bigger V8-powered Glas grand tourer retained its own engine, albeit with a capacity increase to make it a BMW-Glas 3000 V8. Glas' main value to BMW was its Dingolfing assembly plant

Driving Machines

Chapter 7
NEW AND CLASSY

The Sixties undoubtedly saw the beginning of BMW as we know the company today, for they were the years when it finally became profitable again and established a lasting reputation as the world's leading maker of sports saloons. Yet the break with the past was not a clean one: the origins of BMW's recovery lay in the late Fifties, while many of its products during the first half of the Sixties were carryovers from the previous decade.

The models which remained in production as BMW's recovery gathered pace were the Isetta 250 and 300 bubble-cars, which were sold until 1962; the rear-engined 700 economy models, which lasted until 1965; and the big Baroque Angel saloons, which survived until 1964. There was even a short-lived grand tourer, the 3200CS, which was in production from 1962 to 1965 but used the running-gear of the big Fifties saloons. So it was not until 1965 that BMW could really clear the decks and benefit from the new image which the long-awaited medium-sized New Class saloon range of 1962 brought with it.

Towards the end of the previous decade, BMW had been in serious financial trouble. A loan from the Deutsche Bank in 1958 had staved off collapse, but before long the company found itself the target of take-over bids by American Motors and by Britain's Rootes Group, both of which probably saw it as an ideal bridgehead for expansion into continental Europe. In 1959, the company lost 15 million Marks on a turnover of 150 million Marks, and in December that year the Deutsche Bank - its principal creditor - proposed a deal which was effectively a merger with Daimler-Benz. Fortunately for BMW, this proposal was blocked by its shareholders.

Meanwhile, the financiers Harald and Herbert Quandt had been gradually buying BMW shares, and by the middle of 1960 they owned around two-thirds of the entire stock. There was no doubt any more about what would happen to the company. President Heinrich Richter-Brohm resigned, and during 1960 the Quandt brothers pulled in experienced men from Karmann, Borgward and Auto Union to oversee the company's turnaround.

Bertone styled the body of the 3200CS, the grand touring coupe which replaced the 503 for 1962

The BMW Story

The first fruit of the Quandt take-over was the New Class saloon, announced in 1961 but not on sale until 1962. It was a huge success, and BMW exploited its potential through what would now be called niche marketing: Sales Director Paul Hahnemann identified market sectors where there was no direct competition, and Product Planning Director Helmut Bönsch then developed a model specification to suit them. Their success can be gauged from the total of nearly 343,000 New Class saloon models sold over the 10 years of the model's production.

The New Class also spawned two important derivatives. The first was a grand touring coupé to replace the 3200CS. This used the floorpan and running gear of the New Class saloons and survived until a more powerful and facelifted derivative was ready towards the end of the Sixties. The second was the enormously successful '02' range of two-door models, which carried on into the Seventies and are probably the best-liked of the company's Sixties models today. Nearly 843,000 were sold between 1966 and 1974, to make them BMW's unchallenged best-seller.

Production - and profits - soared during the Sixties. In 1966, BMW production exceeded 60,000 cars for the first time ever, and the company was beginning to run out of production capacity. So that year, it bought the Glas company of Dingolfing, with the principal intention of using its factory space to make more BMWs. While plans for this were made ready, however, the company continued to make a limited number of the former Glas models.

As the Sixties came to a close, BMW was poised to take another giant step forwards. The staple engine range of that decade had been the four-cylinder originally drawn up for the New Class cars, but

from 1968 that was joined by a new six-cylinder. From 1969, fuel injection figured among BMW's technological advances. And from the middle of the decade, sales in the USA had really taken off: BMW had cracked its most important overseas market, and from now on there would be no turning back.

The 3200CS

The 3200CS grew out of a proposal by Product Planning Director Helmut Werner Bönsch to replace the expensive 503 as BMW's top-model grand tourer. While examining competitive models in 1960, he realised that the Pininfarina body of the Lancia Flaminia coupé would fit neatly onto the chassis of the Baroque Angel saloons with minimal modifications. So he proposed that BMW should actually build such a car, reasoning that it would be cheaper than the 503.

The BMW Board rejected this idea, but agreed that an Italian-styled coupé on the chassis of the 3200S saloon should replace the 503. So Bertone in Turin was engaged to design and build the car. The Italian stylist came up with one of the most attractive coupés ever to wear BMW badges, although his bodywork was made of steel rather than alloy and the 3200CS was around 100kg heavier than its predecessor. To offset this, the 3.2-litre V8 was uprated to 160bhp and the car could achieve 124mph, against the 503's 118mph. The extra weight did hit acceleration, though.

The prototype 3200CS was on the BMW stand at the 1961 Frankfurt Show, and production began in February 1962. The 3200CS was very much more successful than the 503, finding around twice as many buyers each year as the earlier car. However, it ceased production along with the V8-engined Baroque Angel saloons in

Driving Machines

September 1965. Just 603 cars had been built, of which one was a cabriolet, specially built in 1962 for BMW's Chairman, Herbert Quandt.

Glas and the South African BMW

When BMW bought the Glas concern in 1967, it acquired more than just that company's factories in Dingolfing, about 50 miles from Munich. Although the smaller and cheaper cars - which included the Goggomobil economy car - were dropped, BMW did continue to build two of the Glas coupés at Dingolfing. The Glas 1700GT became a BMW-Glas 1600GT during 1967 when fitted with the 105bhp twin-carburettor engine from the BMW 1600TI, and the Glas 2600 V8 became a BMW-Glas 3000 V8 when BMW carried out Glas' original plan to enlarge its V8 engine. Just 1259 1600GTs and 71 3000 V8s were built with

BMW badges before production was stopped and the Dingolfing plant was turned over to BMW 's own models in 1968.

Meanwhile, a third Glas range was given further life outside Germany. Styled like the two coupés by Frua in Italy, the Glas 1700 was a four-door saloon dating from 1964. BMW shipped its tooling out to Pretoria, where it planned to expand its South African branch into a full manufacturing operation. Fitted with BMW engines and badges, the cars survived in production from 1968 to 1975, by which date around 12,000 had been built. The first models were called the BMW 1800GL; next came the 1800SA; and then from 1970 there was a 2000SA. The original Glas frontal styling was replaced by a BMW front end after 1973, when the cars were renamed the BMW 1804 and 2004.

Glas also made medium-sized saloons, such as this 1.7-litre '1700' model. In 1700TS guise, it had 100bhp and could reach 105mph. BMW fitted its own engines and switched production to South Africa

The BMW Story

The New Class saloons

No question: the New Class saloons were the cars which really saved BMW, after the company had been brought back from the brink by the successful 700 models. The company had needed a medium-sized, volume-produced saloon for years, and this, at last, was it.

Work had begun on such a car in 1955, when Kurt Donath had initiated a project for a four-seater saloon which would have a 1.6-litre slant-four engine - half of the latest 3.2-litre V8. A prototype was running by 1957; there was a re-think in 1958; but in 1960 all work was scrapped after the Quandt take-over, and the project was begun again under Fritz Fiedler. From this time on, it was always called the Neue Klasse (New Class) saloon.

The 700 had pioneered unitary construction and semi-trailing-arm rear suspension at BMW, and both features were retained for the new car. Chassis engineer Eberhard Wolff chose MacPherson strut front suspension (the car was one of the earliest to

have it), backed up by an anti-roll bar to give good handling. Styling and body engineering were entrusted to Wilhelm Hofmeister, and he established a distinctive 'BMW look' for the car, with a low waistline, large glass area, slim roof pillars, flat bonnet and boot and straight-through wing-lines. On the engine side, Alex von Falkenhausen resurrected his 1958 sketches for a 1-litre overhead-camshaft four-cylinder originally intended for the 700 range, and developed these into a 1.5-litre alloy-head masterpiece with built-in stretchability. It was BMW's first four-cylinder car engine since the Thirties.

The BMW 1500 was announced at the Frankfurt Show in autumn 1961, although sales did not begin for another 12 months. The car was universally acclaimed: it was fast, spacious, attractively styled and handled well. Despite its high price, which even in Germany put it head-to-head with the Mercedes-Benz 190 and well above the comparable Opel Rekord and Ford Taunus 17M saloons, it was a huge hit.

The biggest engine fitted to the New Class saloons was a 2-litre four-cylinder. The 2000 had these styled headlights, while lesser variants had round units. The New Class was fundamental to BMW's recovery

Driving Machines

BMW quickly expanded the range, starting with the bored and stroked 1800 in September 1963. More power the following year created the 1800TI (Touring International), and from this a limited run of 200 homologation-special competition cars was created. These were known as the 1800TI/SA (Sportausführung, or Sports Edition).

BMW bored the 1500 engine out in 1964 to create a 1600 which took over from the original model, and then from 1966 the 2000 engine (first seen in the coupés during 1965) was used to create New Class 2000 and 2000TI (twin-carburettor) saloons. The 2-litre models were distinguished by rectangular headlamps and larger horizontal tail-lamp clusters.

The last of the New Class saloons was built in 1972, when the first-generation 5-series (E12) models took over.

The 02 models

As early as 1963, BMW had discussed the possibility of a smaller car with an engine of around 1.4 litres, and after this had been rejected there were also plans to create a smaller version of the Karmann-bodied coupé. Yet neither of these projects seemed to be quite what the company needed, and so instead the engineers focused on a short-wheelbase two-door version of the New Class saloon.

The New Class wheelbase was shortened by two inches, Wilhelm Hofmeister restyled the passenger cabin to suit, the front of the car was given a minor facelift, and a narrow-track rear axle replaced the wide-track type of the four-door cars. For want of a better name, BMW called the two-door 1600-engined car a 1600-2 when it was announced in March 1966.

The two-door '02 range was developed from the four-door New Class. It played a crucial role in re-establishing BMW's sporting credentials, especially in the USA

The BMW Story

Cabriolet derivatives of the 02 were rare. Today, specialists offer a kit to convert saloons. Only the saloon windscreen gives away that this one is a conversion; the real cars had a more raked screen

The 1600-2 was immediately acclaimed as a winner. Its lighter body made it nearly as fast as a four-door 1800, while the handling proved much better. Encouraged, BMW announced a twin-carb 1600ti and a Baur-built cabriolet derivative in 1967.

The 1600 was a big hit in the USA, but new Federal emissions controls debarred the 1600ti. Instead, the company followed importer Max Hoffmann's suggestion and fitted the 2-litre engine, which had

already been certificated for US sales. So, in 1968, the 2002 was born - and that car took the motoring world by storm everywhere it appeared. It was without a doubt the model which made BMW's reputation in the USA, and its success changed the whole future of the company. Over the next six years, it would appear in progressively more powerful forms, going through the twin-carburettor 2002ti, on to the fuel-injected 2002tii and culminating in the 2002 turbo.

The four-cylinder engine in a 2002, best-loved of the 02 range

The 2002 turbo of 1973 was the world's first volume-production turbocharged car, although the 1973-74 Oil Crisis ensured its rarity

Driving Machines

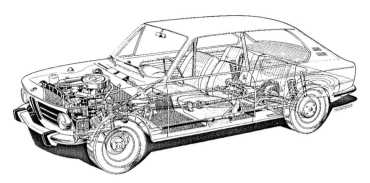

The 02 range was also developed as a hatchback Touring model, years before hatchbacks became fashionable

Meanwhile, BMW had introduced an 1802 model in 1971, together with a three-door body known as the Touring and initially badged 1600, 1800 and 2000 rather than with the '02' numbers which were by now well established. The full cabriolet also became a targa cabriolet in 1971, available only in 2002 form. Then from 1975, there was an entry-level 1502 saloon, initially a response to the 1973-74 fuel crisis but a car which sold astonishingly well alongside the new 3-series saloons which replaced the 02s.

The 02s also had a considerable racing pedigree - see Chapter 8 - and from the need to keep them competitive on the tracks came the idea of turbocharging the 2-litre engine. By 1973, BMW was ready with the roadgoing 2002 turbo, which offered shattering performance but was withdrawn after a year because the oil crisis hit sales of powerful cars.

The 2000 coupés

The 2000 coupé was intended as a cost-effective replacement for the 3200CS, though it was never cheap. 'Chassis' components were borrowed from the New Class saloons, and the coupés were the first cars to have the 2-litre version of the four-cylinder engine. In single-carburettor form, they came as a 2000C and 2000C Automatic; the 2000CS had twin carbs and was sold only with manual transmission.

The body styling was by Wilhelm Hofmeister, and drew heavily on Bertone's style for the 3200CS. So successful was its basic shape that, after a much-needed nose job, it formed the basis of BMW coupé design right up until the arrival of the 6-series in 1976. However, the 2000 coupés were really a stop-gap: cars with their pretensions needed better performance than even the twin-carburettor engine could provide, and it was not until the arrival of the six-cylinder models in 1968 that the concept was properly realised.

The 2000 coupes were blessed with strange front end styling

The BMW Story

For a long time, the R69S was Germany's fastest production motor cycle, with a top speed of 108mph

BMW motorcycles in the Sixties

The motorcycles built by BMW in the Sixties were expensive, refined machines like those the company had always built. Subject to increasing competition from lighter, cheaper, Japanese models, they maintained their image but not their sales.

The touring bike of the period was the R50, seen here in R50S form

The Sixties opened with the big R69 twin getting a hydraulic steering damper and a power increase, while the R27 single took on an articulated frame (like that on the bigger models) and rubber engine mountings. Thereafter, the range gradually shrank. The sports R50S disappeared after 1963, then the R27 and R60 went after 1967. That left the R50 tourer and the R69S as the sporting machine. These two stayed until 1969, when a new generation of bikes was announced.

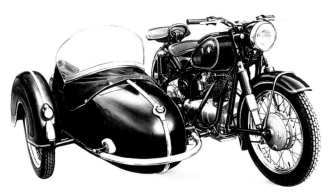

Sidecar enthusiasts chose the R27, seen here with a BMW-badged sidecar

Driving Machines

BRIEF SPECIFICATIONS

BMW 3200CS   Total built: 603

model	period	engine type
3200CS	1962-1965	3168cc V8-cyl, with 160bhp

BMW New Class Saloons   Total built: 342,834

model	period	engine type
1500	1962-1964	1499cc four-cyl, with 80bhp
1600	1964-1966	1573cc four-cyl, with 83bhp
1800	1963-1971	1773cc four-cyl, with 90bhp
1800 Auto	1965-1971	1773cc four-cyl, with 90bhp
1800TI	1964-1966	1773cc four-cyl, with 110bhp
1800TI/SA	1965	1773cc four-cyl, with 130bhp
2000	1966-1972	1990cc four-cyl, with 100bhp
2000 Auto	1966-1972	1990cc four-cyl, with 100bhp
2000TI	1966-1968	1990cc four-cyl, with 120bhp
2000TI Lux	1966-1970	1990cc four-cyl, with 120bhp
2000tii	1969-1972	1990cc four-cyl, with 130bhp

BMW 2000 Coupés   Total built: 13,691

model	period	engine type
2000C	1965-1968	1990cc four-cyl, with 100bhp
2000C Auto	1966-1970	1990cc four-cyl, with 100bhp
2000CS	1965-1970	1990cc four-cyl, with 120bhp

BMW '02 models   Total built: 842,636

model	period	engine type
1600-2	1966-1971	1573cc four-cyl, with 85bhp
1600TI	1967-1968	1573cc four-cyl, with 105bhp
1600 cabriolet	1967-1971	1573cc four-cyl, with 85bhp
1600 Touring	1971-1972	1573cc four-cyl, with 85bhp
1602	1971-1975	1573cc four-cyl, with 85bhp
1802	1971-1975	1766cc four-cyl, with 90bhp
1802 Auto	1971-1975	1766cc four-cyl, with 90bhp
1800 Touring	1971-1974	1766cc four-cyl, with 90bhp
2002	1968-1975	1990cc four-cyl, with 100bhp
2002 Auto	1969-1975	1990cc four-cyl, with 100bhp
2002ti	1968-1971	1990cc four-cyl, with 120bhp
2002tii	1971-1975	1990cc four-cyl, with 130bhp
2002 cabrio	1971-1975	1990cc four-cyl, with 100bhp
2000 Touring	1971-1974	1990cc four-cyl, with 100bhp
2000 Touring Auto	1971-1974	1990cc four-cyl, with 100bhp
2000tii Touring	1971-1974	1990cc four-cyl, with 130bhp
2002 turbo	1973-1974	1990cc four-cyl, with 170bhp
1502	1975-1977	1573cc four-cyl, with 75bhp

Bertone based his Spicup show car on a BMW 2500, fitted with the 2.8-litre big six. Removable panels allowed conversion from open Spider to closed Coupe - hence the name

Smallest-engined of the big coupes was the 2.5CS. Body styling was developed from the four-cylinder 2000C and CS coupes

Driving Machines

Chapter 8
SIX FOR SUCCESS

Nineteen sixty-eight was a milestone year for BMW. Not only was it the year when the company exceeded 500 cars a day for the first time ever, but it was also the year when it introduced two new six-cylinder ranges at the Frankfurt Show.

The company had already turned the corner after the dark days of the Fifties, after its purchase by the Quandt family in 1960 and its successful introduction of the New Class four-door saloons in 1962. These and their two-door '02 derivatives introduced in 1966 sold well enough for BMW to introduce yet more new models and to take on the big guns with them. That meant challenging Mercedes, and it was at Frankfurt in September 1968 that BMW announced the six-cylinder saloons and coupés which would put it back in contention at the top end of the market.

The saloons, developed under the E3 project code, picked up a number of the features which the New Class had introduced seven years earlier. Although their bodyshells were new, they shared the big glass area, crisp lines and forward-sloping front panel of the New Class cars, adding to the latter a neat twin-headlamp installation. Like the smaller models, they also had all-round independent suspension, with MacPherson struts at the front and

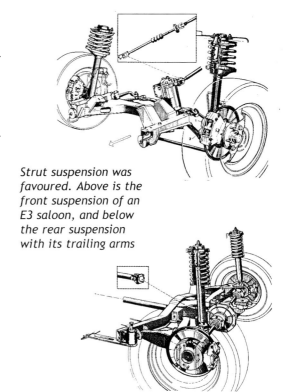

Strut suspension was favoured. Above is the front suspension of an E3 saloon, and below the rear suspension with its trailing arms

semi-trailing arms at the rear, while the principle of an iron-block, alloy-head, SOHC engine installed on the slant to give a low bonnet-line was also a New Class characteristic. The new saloons came in 2500 and 2800 form, the larger engine also with a three-speed automatic option which became available on the 2500 a year later.

The E3 saloons were first with the new six-cylinder engine. This is a 1968 2500

The BMW Story

While the saloons were priced to do battle with Mercedes' 250 and 250SE models, the new E9 coupés took on Mercedes' ageing but newly re-engined 280SE coupés. The BMWs looked fresh, even though they were in fact little more than re-engined and radically face-lifted editions of the rather ugly 2000C and 2000CS models. To fit the six-cylinder engines in, their wheelbases had been stretched by three inches ahead of the passenger cabin, and Wilhelm Hofmeister had designed a new four-lamp nose to give them a family resemblance to the new six-cylinder saloons. In addition, the new saloons' revised front suspension had been added to improve the handling,

engined car with lower equipment levels badged as the BMW Bavaria. Keenly priced at less than the old 2500 had cost, it reversed the E3's fortunes across the Atlantic. Later examples had the ungainly crash bumpers and emissions control equipment demanded by increasingly severe US regulations.

Meanwhile, saloons and coupés alike bene-fited from the new 3-litre engine in 1971. In carburettored form it created the 3.0 S saloon and 3.0 CS coupé (which now had all-disc brakes), while with fuel injection it made the 3.0 Si and 3.0 Csi respectively. And alongside those cars, BMW also intro-duced the low-volume 'homologation spe-

Smart multi-spoke alloy wheels distinguish
a 3-litre-engined coupe from 1971

although the rear axle kept its drum brakes for the time being.

The E3s and E9s were another huge suc-cess for BMW, despite high prices, although US sales of the saloons were slower than the company would have liked. From 1971, however - a year of major change for all the six-cylinder cars - BMW dropped both saloon models from the USA and replaced them with a 2800-

cial' 3.0 CSL coupé, which would go on to confirm the company's growing reputation on the race tracks. The mainstream coupés would remain unchanged until they ceased production in 1975, but the CSL progressed through two further engines - both of them unique - and picked up a whole col-lection of aerodynamic addenda in late 1972 to take on its familiar 'Batmobile' appearance.

Driving Machines

The 3.0CSL 'Batmobile' coupe was a lightweight homologation special, and the majority were sold for competition use.

The next stage came in March 1974, when BMW introduced a long-wheelbase saloon to compete with the long-wheelbase Mercedes luxury limousines. Initially powered by a 3.3-litre version of the six-cylinder engine as a 3.3 L, it became available with the 2.8-litre (2.8 L) and 3-litre (3.0 L) engines a year later. Towards the end of 1976, the 3.3-litre engine was uprated with fuel injection to make the 3.3 Li. The saloons stayed in production a couple of years longer than the coupés, and the last examples came off the assembly lines in 1977. By this time, another revolution in BMW nomenclature was well under way: the New Class cars had given way to 5 Series models, the '02s to the 3 Series, the big coupés had been replaced by 6 Series and the transformation became complete when the first 7 Series cars took over from the six-cylinder saloons.

Key BMW men in the Seventies

In 1967, Harald Quandt was killed in an air crash, and his share in BMW went to his half-brother Herbert Quandt. Herbert brought in the remarkably talented young Eberhard von Kuenheim as his assistant, and appointed him Chairman in 1970. This led to a series of clashes with Sales Director (and, by now, Vice President) Paul Hahnemann, who resigned in October 1971. Hahnemann had done so much for BMW's revival and was so well-liked that the workforce staged a 24-hour strike in protest at the circumstances of his resignation. Quandt quickly brought in Bob Lutz from Opel as Hahnemann's replacement, and it was Lutz who also oversaw the creation of BMW Motorsport GmbH in 1972.

On the design and engineering side, Wilhelm Gieschen was Technical Director after 1963, and Bernhard Osswald came from Ford during the Sixties to replace Fritz Fiedler as R&D chief. Alex von Falkenhausen retired as head of engine design in 1975 and was replaced by Karlheinz Lange. Stylist Wilhelm Hofmeister retired in 1970, and his place was taken by Paul Bracq, who had been Mercedes' chief stylist in the Sixties.

The six-cylinder engine

BMW's 1968 six-cylinder engine was a remarkable achievement, and one which firmly established the company among the world's best car engine makers. The decision to develop what became the M30 engine was taken in 1965, and the project came together under the leadership of Alex von Falkenhausen.

Naturally, the M30 drew on some of the successful features of the four-cylinder

The BMW Story

engine introduced in 1961 for the New Class cars. Thus, it had an iron block and alloy head, a single chain-driven overhead camshaft, and was installed with a slant to give a low bonnet-line. The M30 also had a development of the swirl-inducing combustion chamber first seen on the four-cylinder engine, this time with three 'pockets' in its pentroof design instead of two. BMW called this the Dreikugelwirbelwannenbrennraum, and later added it to the four-cylinder engines as well. Its efficiency allowed the early M30 engines to meet US emissions regulations without the need for an air pump or exhaust gas recirculation equipment.

One of the M30's most notable features was its smoothness throughout a wide rev range. Its seven main bearings were matched by a counterweight on each crank web, and BMW's recent experience with racing engines was put to good use in controlling piston oscillation at high revs. A viscous fan reduced fuel wastage and a special cooling system with one main circuit and two auxiliaries gave faster warm-up and brought other cold-climate benefits.

The M30 engine was developed progressively over the years, switching from twin carburettors to fuel injection with the introduction of the 3003cc variant in 1972 (although 1974's 3295cc type reverted to twin carburettors). By 1975, racing versions of the engine had been stretched to 3453cc and had 24 valves to give 430bhp at 8500rpm. A fuller account of the engine's history is given in Appendix C.

BMW Cars in motorsport

The BMWs most memorably associated with motorsport in this period were the 2002s of the later Sixties and the CSL racing coupés of the early Seventies, but in fact BMW had started looking at motor-sport again as early as 1964. That was when the competition-special 1800TI/SA was made available to privateers. By 1967, the factory was back in business with its own motorsport programme, initially featuring 1600TI models driven by Hubert Hahne and Dieter Quester.

The same two drivers had factory-prepared 2002s for 1968, running in Group 5 of the European Touring Car Championship. Quester won his class that year, and over the next four years the 2002s would win four consecutive German Rally Championship titles. The 2002 finally lost its crown as the top European racing saloon to the Ford Escort. This period also saw competition successes by the tuning firms of Alpina, Heidegger, Koepchen and Schnitzer, who developed racing 2002s to show off their skills in public.

Meanwhile, the CSL coupés had entered motorsport. They did not show well in 1971 or 1972, but became consistent winners in 1973, taking their class at the Le Mans 24-hours among others. The next year was even better, although it was privateers who took CSLs to a win in the European Challenge Cup, and in 1975 it was an Alpina-tuned CSL which won the European Touring Car Championship.

BMW had also been active in Formula 2 racing, providing a variety of engines (all based on production four-cylinders) for a Lola chassis between 1967 and 1971. For 1972, however, BMW Motorsport GmbH was set up with former racing driver Jochen Neerpasch as its manager, and the factory Formula 2 team was disbanded; from now on, BMW would only be a supplier of engines, and the car which had them was a March. In 1972-74, the March-BMW Formula 2 car was a consistent winner, but BMW decided to get out of single-seater racing and farmed out its Formula 2 engine business to Schnitzer in 1976.

Driving Machines

BMW motorcycles in the Seventies

The Seventies opened with a new range of motor cycles from BMW. Actually announced in 1969, the '/5' range had a new, lighter frame with long-travel telescopic front forks. All had the traditional BMW unit construction and shaft drive, and all had flat-twin engines, the R50/5 with 498cc, the R60/5 with 599cc and the R75/5 with 746cc. The new silver paint finish on the R50/5 and R75/5 was a shock to BMW traditionalists, however, accustomed to all-black finishes.

More colours arrived in 1972, when a smaller fuel tank with chromed side panels became standard (although the original 22-litre tank remained available as an option). Longer rear forks improved the handling in 1973, the year when a pair of R75/5s went round the TT circuit for a week to demonstrate their reliability and win the Maudes Trophy.

The new '/6' series bikes took over in 1974, visually similar but with more modern styling of headlamp and instruments. Models were the R60/6 and R75/6, plus two new R90 derivatives with big-bore 898cc engines. The R90/6 was the standard touring bike, while the R90/S was the sports model with a fairing, big fuel tank, twin perforated front disc brakes and stylish paint jobs. These models all lasted until 1976, when the '/7' types took over.

The curved fairing marks this out as an R90/S, the sports model of the '/6' range introduced in 1974

The '/5' models introduced colour to BMW motor cycles. This is an R60/5

The BMW Story

BMW and the turbocharger

When it became clear that the 190bhp 2002 racers were not going to remain competitive for the 1969 season of the European Touring Car Championship, BMW decided to exploit the latitude in the Group 5 rules and to experiment with turbocharging. The original turbocharged racer was a 2002ti with an Eberspacher turbo, and put out 275bhp for a 143mph top speed. In it, Dieter Quester once again won his class in the ETTC, but the turbocharged car was ruled out of Group 5 for 1970, by which time BMW had upped power to 290bhp.

Nevertheless, the possibilities of turbocharging had begun to look exciting, and when BMW unveiled a concept car to mark the opening of its new museum in 1972, the car was known as the BMW Turbo. It was a sleek sports coupé styled by Paul Bracq, with the turbocharged 2-litre engine mounted transversely amidships in its backbone-frame unitary body. BMW claimed 155mph and 0-62mph in 6.6 seconds for this striking-looking machine, which later inspired the fabulous E26 M1 coupés.

There were just two production turbocharged BMWs, the later turbodiesels excepted. These were the 2002 turbo of 1973 and the E23 745i of 1980. The 2002 turbo had just 170bhp and suffered from fearful turbo lag, but it did a great deal for BMW's image as technological leaders. The 745i is covered in Chapter 10.

The Bracq-styled Turbo Coupe of 1972 was a Show special, but built by BMW. It still survives in the BMW Museum, slightly modified after use for aerodynamic experiments

BRIEF SPECIFICATIONS

Note: All engines had six cylinders

The E3 Saloons

Standard (106-inch) wheelbase models

model	period	engine type	built
2500	1968-1977	2494cc, with 150bhp	75,976
2500 Auto	1969-1977	2494cc, with 150bhp	17,387
2800	1968-1975	2788cc, with 170bhp	28,998 *
2800 Auto	1968-1975	2788cc, with 170bhp	11,162 *
3.0 S	1971-1977	2985cc, with 180bhp	29,826
3.0 S Auto	1971-1977	2985cc, with 180bhp	21,718
3.0 Si	1971-1977	2985cc, with 200bhp	19,724
3.0 Si Auto	1971-1977	2985cc, with 200bhp	2586

Total built   207,377

* Figures for US-model BMW Bavaria are included in these totals.

Long (110-inch) wheelbase models

model	period	engine type	built
2.8 L	1975-1977	2788cc, with 170bhp	3423
2.8 L Auto	1975-1977	2788cc, with 170bhp	1613
3.0 L	1975-1977	2985cc, with 180bhp	2529
3.0 L Auto	1975-1977	2985cc, with 180bhp	2992
3.3 L	1974-1976	3295cc, with 190bhp	381
3.3 L Auto	1974-1976	3295cc, with 190bhp	1241
3.3 Li	1976-1977	3205cc, with 197bhp	477
3.3 Li Auto	1976-1977	3205cc, with 197bhp	924

Total built: 12,656

The E9 Coupés

model	period	engine type	built
2.5 CS	1974-1975	2494cc, with 150bhp	844
2800CS	1968-1971	2788cc, with 170bhp	6924
2800CS Auto	1969-1971	2788cc, with 170bhp	2475
3.0 CS	1971-1975	2985cc, with 180bhp	5017
3.0 CS Auto	1971-1975	2985cc, with 180bhp	5071
3.0 CSi	1971-1975	2985cc, with 200bhp	8142
3.0 CSL	1971-1975	3153cc, with 206bhp	1096

Total built: 29,569

The BMW Story

Paul Bracq's styling for the E21 3 Series gave the cars a strong family resemblance to the larger E12s. In this view, note particularly the shape of the rear window, the bumper wraparounds, and the side rubbing-strips

Driving Machines

Chapter 9
FIVES AND THREES

BMW had started to expand in the middle of the Sixties, beginning with its purchase of Glas in 1967. That was very nearly followed by the purchase of Lancia in 1968 - but BMW was pipped at the post by Fiat - and the early years of the Seventies witnessed further expansion in all directions. Between 1970 and 1972, the Munich, Landshut and Dingolfing plants were all increased in size, and by the middle of the decade, BMW was building 1000 cars a day, a volume unimaginable when the business had been bought up by the Quandt family just 15 years earlier.

Nor was that all. Towards the end of 1971, a new proving ground was opened at Aschheim. During 1972, BMW opened its new Motorsport division and built a museum complex in Munich together with a spectacular new administrative headquarters - the latter close enough to the Olympic Stadium to give the company free publicity every time the stadium appeared on worldwide TV during that year's Olympics. In 1974, BMW established its own assembly plant in South Africa, and the following year it set up a branch in the USA.

All these changes were of course the fruit of the success which had finally come to the company during the Sixties, and the new model-ranges of the Seventies would build further on that success. A new marketing strategy would also be put in place, and the rather confused model-ranges of the Sixties would give way to a clear and strict pecking-order. The smallest two-door cars would be called the 3 Series; the four-door saloons would be called the 5 Series; right at the top would be 7 Series luxury saloons; and discreetly below them would be 6 Series luxury coupés. However, it would be some years before this new strategy was fully in place, and the last stage - the 7 Series big saloons, would not be implemented until 1977. In the meantime, the different model-ranges still appeared confusing to an outsider.

The first of the new ranges to arrive was the 5 Series, which replaced the four-door saloons of the New Class in 1972. Developed under the project code of E12, the 5 Series is perhaps best understood as a radical evolution from the New Class. The first cars shared a lot of their running-gear with the New Class, although their bodyshells were completely new and had been developed with passenger safety very much in mind. New mechanical elements were of course introduced as the years passed.

The sleek lines of the E12 were almost certainly influenced by Bertone's 1970 design exercise on the 2002ti. This is a 525 model

The BMW Story

The E12s were announced at the Munich Olympics in September 1972, and the first cars were 2-litre four-cylinder models, the 520 with a carburettored engine and the much more expensive 520i with fuel injection. Both used engines derived from those in the New Class cars, the 2000 and 2000tii respectively. The range expanded quickly, embracing a six-cylinder 525 in 1973 (which took its engine from the 2500) and a 518 in 1974 to meet demand for smaller-engined cars after the 1973-74 oil crisis.

All models had a minor facelift in 1976, and then the 520 became a six-cylinder model with the introduction of the new 2-litre 'small six' in September 1977. After 1975, the top model was a 528 (with the 2800's engine) until a 528i superseded it in 1977. Five-speed gearboxes arrived in 1978-79, with a choice on some models of overdrive or close-ratio types. For the USA there was also a 530i, and for the fortunate few a formidable M535i from the Motorsport division after 1979. Even rarer was the Alpina 3.3-litre conversion.

Production of all remaining models stopped in 1981.

The build quality of the 5-series and its excellent combination of handling and per-

The E12 range was a revelation in the 1970s: a family saloon with excellent handling and sporting performance

Early E12s had a flat bonnet, as on this 520

Driving Machines

The 1976 facelift gave more shape to the E12's bonnet and made the grille appear taller. It also reinforced the resemblance to the then-new E21...

formance with the space and comfort of a family saloon quickly earned it worldwide respect. In Britain, these were the cars which really put BMW on the map for the middle-class motorist, the 528i in particular becoming a highly-regarded middle-class status symbol.

All the 5 Series cars were built at Dingolfing, the former Glas factory which had been re-tooled specially for their assembly. Their engines, however, were made at the Munich plant which built engines for all the other BMWs of the time - including the new E21 3 Series cars which came to replace the much-loved '02 two-door models during 1975. These were assembled at the Milbertshofen plant.

The '02 range had clearly defined the market position for the new 3 Series range, and the cars slipped neatly in as replacements - although BMW went on to expand their appeal far beyond that of the '02 cars. The E21s were styled by Paul Bracq and were slightly bigger and heavier than the cars they replaced. They also had a strong family likeness to the bigger 5 Series models. The 316, 318, 320 and 320i announced in July 1975 all had modified versions of the four-cylinder engines familiar from the '02 cars, and their overall chassis layout was very similar.

However, front suspension had been modified to reflect E3 (2500/2800/3.0) saloon practice, there were ventilated disc brakes

...which is pictured here. Indicator details differed, of course, and the four-cylinder E21s had single headlamps

The BMW Story

at the front even though the rear axle still had drums, and the E21s re-introduced rack-and-pinion steering to the BMW line-up. (It had last been seen on the rear-engined 700 and LS models a decade earlier.) Four-speed gearboxes were standard, but buyers could pay extra for a five-speed Getrag 'box or for a three-speed ZF automatic, the latter on all models except the 316.

Spirited driving could provoke quite nasty oversteer in these new small BMWs, but the buyers loved them and soon demanded more performance. BMW gave it to them in September 1977 in the shape of two six-cylinder models: a 320 to replace the four-

cylinder 320 and 320i, and a 323i to top the range off. The 323i proved a hugely desirable little road-burner, although it seemed to suffer even more than the other E21s from rear-end breakaway.

The engines in these two cars were entirely new, and the 2-litre version went into the 520 at the same time. Essentially, BMW had found insufficient room in the E21's engine bay for its existing six-cylinder engine, and had therefore decided to develop a new small-block six, which would have further applications in the future. The M60 engine had a lot in common with the older and larger six, but it was particularly notable for its lightweight

Six-cylinder E21s were distinguished from four-cylinder models by their twinned headlamps

Driving Machines

construction (despite a cast-iron block) and cogged-belt camshaft drive instead of the chain-drive used on other BMW engines.

Among the '02 range which the E21s replaced had been a low-volume Targa-top cabriolet, and BMW decided to offer a similar edition of its new car. About 3000 3 Series Targas were built by Baur in Stuttgart, but they were not sold in all BMW's markets and could not be had with the six-cylinder engines.

The E21 3 Series proved another runaway success for BMW, its crisp styling and modern interior (complete with dashboard angled towards the driver) perfectly reflecting the aspirations of the times. In Britain, it proved an ideal complement to the 5-series, attracting younger buyers to the marque and successfully retaining their loyalty when the time came to trade up.

BMW broke its own production records over and over again during the Seventies, thanks mostly to the success of the 3 Series and 5 Series saloons. In 1976, the company built just over 275,000 cars; for 1977, the figure just exceeded 290,000;

and in 1978 more than 320,000 new BMWs were built. The E21 3 Series went on to achieve an astonishing 1.37 million units before it was finally taken out of production in the early Eighties and replaced by the second-generation 3 Series or E30. That made it BMW's best-ever seller ... for a time.

BMW people

The BMW family continued to change around in the early Seventies. Claus Luthe came from Audi to take over from Paul Bracq as head of styling in 1974, and Hans-Erdmann Schönbeck also left Audi to replace Bob Lutz as sales chief. Karlheinz Radermacher had joined BMW as understudy to R&D man Bernhard Osswald in 1973, and in 1975 took over when Osswald retired.

BMW in South Africa

In order to get around the huge import duties levied by the South African government, BMW had started building cars in South Africa as early as 1968. The first cars were actually rebadged Glas models, built from the Glas tooling which BMW had shipped out to Pretoria. However, produc-

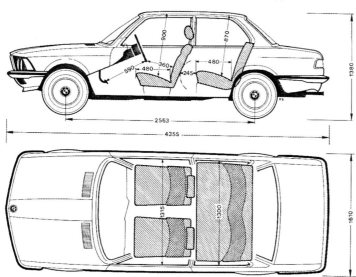

Interior dimensions of the E21s were adequate for a compact sporting saloon, but rear seat leg room was limited

The BMW Story

tion of these ceased in 1975 and BMW began to build E12 5 Series cars at a new assembly plant established at Rosslyn, in the Cape. This was supplied with cars sent out CKD (Completely Knocked Down, or in kit form) from Germany.

The first South African 5 Series cars were 520s, 525s and 528s assembled in 1974. More than 53,000 E12s were assembled at the Rosslyn plant for sale in African countries before production switched to the E28 5 Series in the early Eighties. From 1977, Rosslyn also assembled 3 Series cars, and just over 8500 examples of the E21 came off the lines there.

Fives and Threes in the USA

Since the Fifties, BMWs had reached American customers through the Hoffmann Motors Corporation, a major import concern which handled several European marques. Its head, Max Hoffmann, had wielded considerable influence over the cars which BMW had developed for sale across the Atlantic. However, all that changed in March 1975, when BMW set up its own US headquarters in Montvale, New Jersey, and established its own dealership network.

US customers had to wait until late 1974 to get a 5 Series saloon, and then the one they got was quite different from the European models. Emissions control regulations sapped so much power that BMW had decided to equip it with a larger-capacity engine than in any European E12 of the time. So the 530i had a 176bhp edition of the 2982cc six-cylinder engine used in the 3.0 CSL coupé. It also had marker lights on the front wing corners and some ugly extended bumpers to meet the 5mph collision regulations.

The 530i went down a storm in the USA, and Road and Track magazine chose it as one of the world's top ten cars. It lasted until 1979, when an emissions-controlled version of the 528i replaced it. US customers grumbled about the name change, the smaller capacity engine and the lower output of 171bhp, but the car was actually faster as well as more fuel-efficient than the 530i.

As for the 3 Series, the only variant to make it to the USA was the 320i, and that stayed with the four-cylinder engine even after European 320s had gone to six cylinders in 1977. The original car went on sale during 1976, with its 2-litre engine fitted with air injection and exhaust gas recirculation equipment to give 110bhp in 49-state Federal tune and 105bhp with the additional constraints required in California. Suspension alterations on 1978 models helped to tame the oversteer which afflicted early cars, and then the 1980 models switched to the 1766cc engine, although they still retained 320i badges. These later cars had five-speed gearboxes and a lower final drive; their 101bhp engines were less flexible than the earlier 2-litres but were more economical and smoother thanks to the use of a catalytic converter instead of the earlier type of emissions control equipment.

A 5 Series forerunner

The Italian styling house of Bertone built a special show-car on the basis of a BMW 2002ti in 1970. While the rather gimmicky interior was fortunately ignored by BMW, the exterior most definitely had an influence on the shape of the 5 Series cars introduced just two years later. Whether the car was in fact commissioned as part of the E12 5 Series development programme is something on which the history books are still not clear today, although the Bertone car did have only two doors, whereas the 5-series was always planned as a four-door...

The E12 5 Series

All models had four doors and a wheelbase of 103.8 inches. These specifications are for European cars. Production totals are approximate.

model	period	engine type	built
Four-cylinder models			
518	1974-1981	1766cc, with 90bhp at 5500rpm	125,000
520	1972-1977	1990cc, with 115 at 5800	(520 &
520i	1972-1975	1990cc, with 130 at 5800; Kugelfischer injection	520i)
	1975-1977	1990cc, with 125 at 5700; Bosch injection	140,000
Six-cylinder models			
520	1977-1981	1990cc, with 122bhp at 6000rpm	150,000
525	1973-1976	2494cc, with 145 at 6000; Two Zenith carbs	
	1976-1981	2494cc, with 150 at 5800; Single Solex carb	130,000
528	1975-1976	2788cc, with 165 at 5800; Two Zenith carbs	
	1976-1977	2788cc, with 170 at 5800; Single Solex carb	(528
528i	1977-1978	2788cc, with 176 at 5800	& 528i)
	1978-1981	2788cc, with 184 at 5800	110,000
M535i	1979-1981	3453cc, with 218 at 5200	1410

In addition, approximately 27,870 530i models were built, and approximately 53,500 E12 saloons were assembled in South Africa from CKD kits.

Grand total: 738,000 approximately

THE E21 3-SERIES

All models had two doors and a wheelbase of 100.9 inches. These specifications are for European cars.

model	period	engine type
Four-cylinder models		
315	1981-1983	1573cc, with 75bhp at 5800rpm
316	1975-1980	1563cc, with 90bhp at 6000rpm
	1980-1982	1766cc, with 90bhp at 5500rpm
318	1975-1980	1754cc, with 98bhp at 5800rpm
318i	1980-1982	1766cc, with 105bhp at 5800rpm
320	1975-1977	1977cc, with 109bhp at 5800rpm
320i	1975-1977	1977cc, with 125bhp at 5700rpm
Six-cylinder models		
320	1977-1982	1990cc, with 122bhp at 6000rpm
323i	1978-1982	2315cc, with 143bhp at 6000rpm

BMW provides production totals by calendar year and not by individual model. The E21s were built in the following quantities:

1975	43,349	1980	204,358 + 1968 CKD = 206,326	
1976	130,821	1981	226,960 + 1872 CKD = 228,832	
1977	166,218 + 540 CKD = 166,758	1982	181,254 + 756 CKD = 182,010	
1978	182,213 + 1164 CKD = 183,377	1983	33,349 + 408 CKD = 33,757	
1979	186,973 + 1836 CKD = 188,809		**Grand total: 1,364,039**	

Top of the range from 1980 was the turbocharged 745i. This E23 variant never sold quite as strongly as BMW had hoped, but 16,031 found customers in just over six years

Driving Machines

Chapter 10
POWER, PRESTIGE AND PERFORMANCE

BMW's determined assault on the luxury saloon and luxury coupé markets continued in the mid-Seventies as first the E24 6 Series coupés and then the E23 7 Series saloons were announced. Their new names followed the style established earlier in the decade by the mid-range 5 Series and compact 3 Series saloons, and made the hierarchy of the BMW model-ranges much easier to understand. Customers felt much more comfortable, knowing that their 728i was clearly marked out as a more expensive model than the 528i which shared the same engine; it was all much easier to comprehend than in the days of the 2002, the 2000CS and the 3.3Li!

The 6 Series coupés were the first to appear, and were announced at the Geneva Show in March 1976. They rode on a slightly shortened version of the 5 Series saloon floorpan, but incorporated a modified rear suspension which would also be seen in the big 7 Series saloons. The 6 Series was also the first BMW to feature speed-proportional power-assisted steering, and it introduced the Active Check Control monitoring system and on-board computer to the BMW range.

Design work on the 6 Series had started in 1973, under Bernhard Osswald, and had been completed under his successor Karlheinz Radermacher. The body styling was by Paul Bracq, whose sure touch produced an elegant car with a broad and purposeful stance and a strong family resemblance to the E9 CS coupés it was to replace. With the exception of additional spoilers and a modified rear bumper wrap-around (the latter in 1982), that styling remained unchanged during a production run of 16 years - and the 6 Series looked just as much the wealthy man's grand tourer in 1989 as it had done on its introduction. The 6 Series bodies were always built by Karmann of Osnabrück, who also assembled the cars for their first year of production. However, quality control on these early models was not all it might have been, and BMW moved assembly to its own Dingolfing plant in August 1977.

The first 6 Series models were the carburettored 630CS and the fuel injected 633 CSi, both of them using versions of the engines seen in the superseded E9 coupés. The bigger-engined car was certainly no slouch - but it was not as quick as the

The big coupes of this period were the E24 6-series models, represented here by a 630CS

The BMW Story

The 6 Series cars all had one or other variant of the big six-cylinder engine. This is a 630CS or 633CSi, the latter initially the top model

Mercedes 450 SLC 5.0. So BMW's Chairman Eberhard von Kuenheim instructed his engineers to go one better, and the result was the 635 CSi. Announced in July 1978, this had a new five-speed gearbox as standard and a purposeful-looking black rubber tail spoiler which helped to differentiate it from the lesser models. Its M-90 engine was a much-detuned version of the 3453cc unit seen in the racing CSLs, and made the 635 CSi into a genuine 140mph car. This allowed BMW to claim that it built the fastest four-seater coupé in Europe - as long as the Porsche 928 was classified as a 2+2 rather than a proper four-seater!

From 1978, the 635CSi was the top model, and from 1983 there was the Motorsport-developed M635CSi. The discreet tail spoiler distinguishes the big-engined version of the coupe

Driving Machines

Things were not quite so comfortable for BMW over in the USA, where the exchange rate pumped up the already high prices of the 6 Series cars. The first examples to cross the Atlantic were 630 CSi models - essentially the European 630 CS with extended 'safety' bumpers and with fuel injection to give more precise control of exhaust emissions. These were introduced early in 1977 and lasted just one year, being replaced for 1978 by the more torquey (but no more powerful) Federalised 633 CSi. The 635 CSi never did make it to the USA.

The carburettored 630 CS was dropped in August 1979, and in its stead came a 628 CSi which offered the same power and performance with greater fuel economy from a high-compression version of the injected 2.8-litre engine in the 528i. All 6 Series were now fuel injected, the Bosch L-Jetronic system being used at first although BMW gradually switched to the even more sophisticated Motronic system which featured mapped injection and ignition. The 3.5-litre models meanwhile showed up well in European Touring Car Championship events, and as a direct result BMW's Motorsport division announced the special high-performance M 635 CSi derivative in 1983 (featured later in this chapter).

To meet new German regulations which offered tax advantages to motorists who went 'green', catalytic converters became optional on the 3.5-litre models in September 1985. The final changes then came in May 1987, when the 628 CSi disappeared from the range, bumpers were modified and front spoilers gained integral driving lamps, and twin-tube gas dampers were standardised. The last 6 Series coupés were built early in 1989, but BMW did not replace these big Autobahn-stormers directly. There was a decent interval before the E31 8 Series coupés arrived in 1990 - and they were rather different cars in a number of ways.

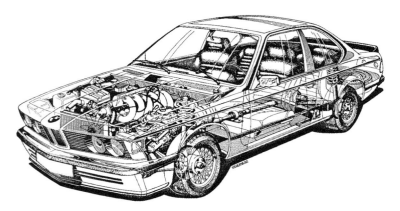

The 3.5-litre coupes had a squarer chin spoiler, as shown on this cutaway

The 6 Series may have been a big car, but it was definitely a 2+2. Rear seat passengers had less room than in a 3 Series saloon

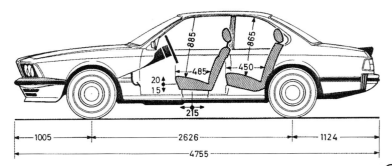

The BMW Story

If the 6 Series coupés had been deliberately aimed at stealing sales from Mercedes-Benz, the 7 Series flagship saloons announced in January 1977 were in an even more obvious head-to-head contest. This time, their targets were the Mercedes W116 S-Class saloons (and, from 1979, their W126 replacements). In most respects, they succeeded only too well, although the cars did acquire an early reputation for problems. It used to be said in Germany that the car most likely to be seen broken down at the side of an Autobahn was a first-generation 7-series BMW.

The original project for a new flagship saloon had been initiated shortly after the E3 (2500/2800) models had gone on sale in 1968, but was aborted when the 1973 fuel crisis caused a rethink of future strategy at BMW. Greater emphasis was accorded to fuel economy and weight-saving in the new E23 project, and this was combined with the search for greater comfort and greater safety. Nevertheless, the design for the E23 was settled early in 1976 and the first cars appeared a year later.

Where the E3s had come in short- and long-wheelbase forms, the E23s came only as long-wheelbase cars. Their styling, by Paul Bracq, echoed his successful work on the E12 5-series cars, although a more pointed nose helped to distinguish the bigger saloons at a glance. The first models were carburettor 728s and 730s, with an injected 733i - all using basically the same engines as the superseded E3s. Two years later, the carburettor models were dropped in favour of injected types, and a new 735i model was introduced with the 3430cc M90 engine which gave 135mph performance. At the same time, Motronic engine management changed the 733i into a 732i.

There was even more exciting news in 1980, when BMW introduced its 745i super-saloon to combat Mercedes' new 500SE and 500SEL models. Originally planned to have a V12 engine (see page 086), this actually had a turbocharged version of the 3210cc big six which gave it a 138mph maximum and a 0-60mph time of less than 8 seconds. The car never sold quite as well as BMW had hoped, but was improved in

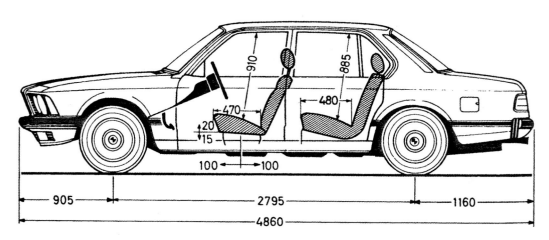

The E23 saloons offered the generous interior space expected of a luxury car

Driving Machines

The long wheelbase so important for ride comfort in the E23 saloons is clear in this picture

1983 with better fuel economy and more torque from a Motronic-equipped 3430cc engine.

Reworked front ends and a 250lb. weight trimming operation improved fuel economy across the board in 1982, and the three-speed ZF automatic was replaced by a new four-speed ZF type with torque converter lockup in top gear. The four remaining models - 728i, 732i, 735i and 745i - gained ABS as standard during 1984 and remained available until the range was replaced by the second-generation E32 7 Series cars in May 1986.

E23s also had the 3.5-litre six, as this cutaway of a 735i demonstrates

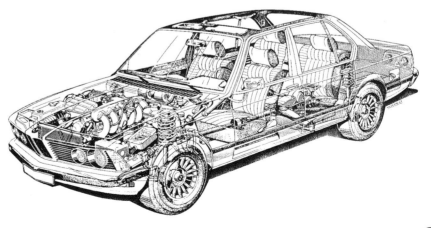

The BMW Story

The V12 that might have been

It was some time around 1971 when BMW started work on a V12 engine intended for eventual use in its flagship saloons. The basis of the engine was two 2.3-litre M60 small-block sixes on a common crankshaft. However, the project was put on hold after the 1973 energy crisis and had been formally abandoned by 1978. In its place, Karlheinz Lange's engine designers developed the turbocharged six which eventually appeared in the 745i.

not actually available until the following spring, the M635 CSi was the result.

The M635 CSi was powered by a further development of the four-valve 3453cc M-88 engine used in the M1, now with Bosch Motronic engine management. It achieved an astonishing 286bhp at 6500rpm and would rev freely right to its 8000rpm limit. When Autocar and Motor tried an M635 CSi in 1989, 60mph came up in 6 seconds, 100mph in just over 15 seconds, and the car reached its maximum 150mph at

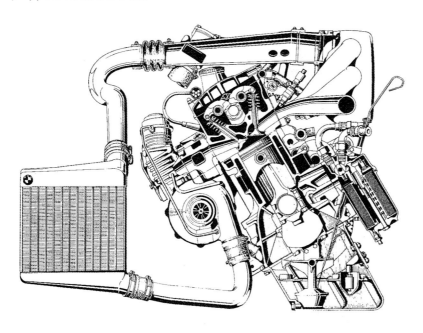

A turbocharged version of the 3.5-litre engine was used in the 745i after cancellation of the V12. Note the intercooler on the left

The M635 CSi

BMW's Motorsport division had opened for business in 1972, and had already distinguished itself by means of the M1 from 1978 and the M535i from 1979. Although BMW was not fielding a works team in the early Eighties, the success of privateers driving tuned 635 CSi cars in the European Touring Car Championship was a good enough excuse for the Motorsport division to develop its own high-performance 6 Series model from 1983. Announced at the September 1983 Frankfurt Show, but

6200rpm - all of them astonishing figures for a big and heavy coupé.

The M635 CSi was remarkably sure-footed, although its ride could be a little harsh and its engine was not as refined as many customers had come to expect from BMW's big sixes. Even so, the car was a motoring classic from the moment it arrived. Just 5803 examples were sold to lucky customers between 1984 and 1989. The car is nowadays often known as an M6, the name which was given to it in the USA.

The 6 Series in motorsport

The 3.5-litre 6 Series cars made a name for themselves in the European Touring Car Championship in the Eighties. The first ones to take to the track were three Group 2 635 CSi models, prepared by Rudi Eggenberger in Switzerland for the 1981 Championship. With 370bhp, they put up a good performance, but could not beat the Porsches. Then in 1983, the new Group A regulations demanded cars which were closer to standard, and there were teams of 635 coupés from the tuners Alpina, Schnitzer and Juma. That year, BMW won the ETCC against stiff opposition from the V12-engined Jaguars.

Weight ultimately counted against the big BMWs, but the cars were still winning ETCC events in the mid-Eighties, once again prepared by the aftermarket tuners.

Supercar or fiasco? The M1

The M1 had its origins in BMW's desire to tackle Porsche in international sports car racing and to build a car which would expand the BMW marque into supercar territory. The concept came from Jochen Neerpasch, head of the Motorsport division, and the inspiration for its realisation from the 1972 mid-engined BMW Turbo show coupé.

BMW originally planned to build a limited run of 450 cars. Rather than use up valuable space in its own assembly halls, the German company decided to sub-contract assembly to a specialist - and it hit upon Lamborghini to do the job. Unfortunately, Lamborghini took rather longer to gear up for production than BMW had hoped, and before the M1 was announced at the 1978 Paris Show, BMW had cancelled the assembly contract and given it to the coach-builder Baur in Stuttgart.

The M1 was thus late - and by the time it was ready, racing regulations had changed and the proposed Group 5 racer (a 'silhouette' car which bore little resemblance to the production M1 except in its shape) was no longer viable. A tentative switch to Group 6 showed that the M1 was not competitive. Fortunately, Neerspach came to the rescue, dreaming up the Procar series with Max Moseley. This series, conceived as curtain-raisers to European Grands Prix, allowed privateers to compete against professional Formula One drivers in identically-prepared M1s. Despite a mass of political difficulties, the Procar series ran successfully for the 1979 and 1980 seasons, and did a lot of good in promoting the BMW image.

However, BMW did not prolong the agony. Just 457 M1s were built between 1978 and 1981, 397 of them as road cars and the other 60 as competition machines. Their rarity and consequent value as collector's items kept them off the race-tracks after the Procar series ended. In addition, a few prototypes were built by Lamborghini in 1977-1978.

The M1 project was beset with problems in the beginning, but the car did much good for BMW's image

The BMW Story

The M1 was built around a hefty tubular space-frame (designed to withstand the stresses imposed by the planned Group 5 700bhp turbocharged engine). Like the 1972 BMW Turbo, it had its engine mounted amidships for optimum weight distribution and was conceived as a two-seater coupé. Giorgio Giugiaro's Ital Design company was commissioned to do the styling, and the engine was a 277bhp four-valve version of the 3453cc Motorsport M-88, with Kugelfischer mechanical fuel injection.

BMW motorcycles, 1976-1986

The decade which followed BMW's introduction of the '/7' motor cycles in 1976 was an eventful one for the marque. It saw the arrival of the first integral touring fairing (on the 1976 R100RS) and the first BMW trail bike (the 1981 R80 G/S); it saw the introduction of 'monolever' swinging-arm rear suspension, and it also saw the end of 60 unbroken years of flat-twin BMW motor cycles with unit gearboxes.

The period began with the biggest flat-twin being enlarged to 980cc for the R100

models and the R60 and R75 becoming /7 types. The R75/7 became a 797cc R80/7 in 1977, and then 1978 saw two new entry-level models in the shape of the 473cc R45 and 650cc R65.

Major changes came in 1981, when the R80 G/S took BMW into the fashionable trail bike market and pioneered the monolever rear suspension. Over the next couple of years, there were detail modifications but by 1983 the range still consisted of four basic types - the R45, R65, R80 and R100 - all available with different equipment levels. The R100RT touring bike even had Boge Nivomat self-levelling rear suspension.

Then in 1983 BMW introduced the new K Series range, three models with the same fuel-injected twin overhead-camshaft 987cc four-cylinder engine mounted on its side facing north-south. The K100s all had five-speed gearboxes and shaft drive, with monolever rear suspension and cast alloy wheels. In 1984, they replaced the R100 range, and over the next couple of years the remaining /7 models gradually acquired the monolever suspension.

This is the R60/7 motor cycle, made between 1976 and 1980

The R100RS was the first BMW motor cycle with an integral fairing

Driving Machines

The E24 6 Series

All models had two doors and a wheelbase of 103.4 inches. All engines had six cylinders.

model	period	cc; bhp at rpm	engine type
628 CSi	1979-1987	2788; 184/5800	Bosch L-Jetronic injection
630 CS	1976-1979	2985; 185/5800	Single Solex 4A1 carburettor
633 CSi	1976-1982	3210; 197/5500	Bosch L-Jetronic injection
635 CSi	1978-1981	3453; 218/5200	Bosch L-Jetronic injection
635 CSi	1982-1987	3430; 218/5200	Bosch Motronic management
635 CSi KAT	1987-1989	3430; 211/5700	Bosch Motronic management
M635 CSi	1983-1989	3453; 286/6500	Bosch Motronic management; Twin overhead camshafts and four valves per cylinder

The M1

Two-door models with a wheelbase of 100.8 inches.

period	cc	bhp at rpm	engine type
1978-1981	3453	277/6500	Kugelfischer mechanical injection; Twin overhead camshafts and four valves per cylinder

The E23 7 Series

All models had four doors and a wheelbase of 110 inches. All engines had six cylinders.

model	period	cc; bhp at rpm	engine type
728	1977-1979	2788; 170/5800	Single Solex 4A1 carburettor
728i	1979-1986	2788; 184/5800	Bosch L-Jetronic fuel injection
730	1977-1979	2985; 184/5800	Single Solex 4A1 carburettor
732i	1979-1982	3205; 197/5500	Bosch Motronic management
733i	1977-1979	3205; 197/5500	Bosch L-Jetronic fuel injection
735i	1979-1982	3453; 218/5200	Bosch L-Jetronic injection (to July 1980) Bosch Motronic (from August 1980)
735i	1982-1986	3420; 218/5200	Bosch Motronic management
745i	1980-1982	3205; 252/5200	Bosch L-Jetronic injection and KKK turbocharger
745i	1983-1986	3430; 252/4900	Bosch Motronic management and KKK turbocharger

Production totals

All 6 Series cars were built in Germany. More than 15,000 of the total 7 Series cars were built at the Rosslyn plant in South Africa; these included examples of all types except the 745i.

6 Series:	86,216	
7 Series:	285,368	including Rosslyn production
M1:	457	

The BMW Story

The E28 was the second-generation 5 Series introduced in 1981.
This 525i reveals its stylish but essentially conservative lines

Driving Machines

Chapter 11
SYMBOLS OF THEIR TIMES

The Eighties was the decade when everything came together for BMW. The company had been building fine cars for many years, but those cars had mostly appealed to a particularly discerning breed of motorist. If the company was to grow, it had to broaden its appeal - and yet it was vital not to lose the essential BMW qualities on which the marque had built its reputation.

BMW was well up to the challenge. The new cars of the Eighties were astonishingly competent machines which looked good, had first-rate build quality, and actually enhanced the marque's sporting qualities. Clever marketing enabled the buyer of the humblest 316 to believe that his car was a close relative of the giant-killing M3s and M5s, and as the Eighties wore on, so a

BMW became a symbol of the age.

The Eighties was of course the heyday of the Yuppies (Young, Upwardly-Mobile Professionals), and BMW suffered something of an image problem in some quarters when its cars became very closely associated with that section of the community. But the cars were above that, and the second-generation 3 Series (E30) and second-generation 5 Series (E28) are now regarded not only as modern classics but as outstanding cars of their time. The later Eighties saw the E28s replaced by a third-generation 5 Series, the E34 which remained in production until the mid-Nineties; and those cars are as desirable now as they were on their introduction in 1988.

Seen here as a cutaway is a 535i of the third-generation 5 Series or E34 range. These remarkably competent cars made their bow in 1988

The BMW Story

The first of the Eighties BMWs was the E28 5 Series, introduced in June 1981 with a restricted four-model range which later expanded to include the company's first diesel saloons and Motorsport variants in the shape of the M535i and the formidable M5. Many people thought the E28s were disappointingly similar to the E12s they replaced, but there was no denying that their slicker lower-body styling - on a slightly shorter wheelbase - modernised a shape which had begun to look dated.

The E28 models featured the characteristic BMW 'face', with a forward-sloping grille

Selectable automatic transmissions made their appearance in this period. This is in an M535i

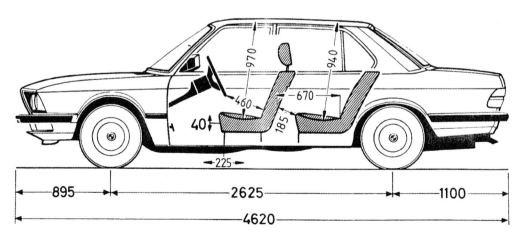

Despite quite generous interior dimensions, the E28s were not particularly big cars

Driving Machines

The E34 version of the M5 was a hugely desirable Q-car, with family practicality allied to blistering performance

The second-generation 3 Series or E30 models were the next to appear, being announced in November 1982 although deliveries did not actually begin until early in 1983. Once again, BMW had settled for evolution rather than revolution in their styling (a policy the company maintains to this day), and perhaps the most significant

The E30 3 Series cars introduced in 1982 had the quite angular styling typical of the 1980s

The BMW Story

change was that the two-door models were quickly supplemented by four-door saloons in order to tackle the challenge of Mercedes' new 'compact' 190E saloon. A Baur-built Targa-top body available from the beginning carried on the tradition of the older 3 Series, but it gave way to an extremely pretty full cabriolet from 1986. Then 1987 saw the body range expanded still further with the first touring estates, which were undeniably stylish but rather less practical than they appeared.

Naturally, there was a high-performance M3 derivative as well, available from 1986 as a saloon and then between May 1988 and June 1991 as a cabriolet. Only 800 of these open-air M3s were built, and even fewer of the homologation-special M3 Sport Evolution announced in December 1990. By that date, in fact, the E36 replacement range had been announced,

and E30 saloon production came to an end in April 1991. The cabriolets lingered until December 1993 and the touring estates until 1995.

Last of the Eighties ranges to appear was the E34 5 Series, although its late arrival made it strictly a car of the early Nineties. Announced in January 1988, it was very similar visually to the recently-introduced E32 7 Series and represented a great step forward from the E28 it replaced. The longer wheelbase made for much better ride comfort, and the new styling lent itself extraordinarily well to a touring estate version announced in 1991. From July 1992, the traditional top-of-the-range big sixes were replaced by 3-litre and 4-litre V8s from the 7 Series, although the high-performance M5 retained its large-capacity six-cylinder engine to the end.

This two-door E30 from 1986 is equipped with the optional M-Technik front spoiler

Driving Machines

The Eighties and early Nineties saw some interesting technical developments which affected all BMW cars. The earliest of these was the introduction of four-wheel drive as an option on the E30 models (see 'The X-Cars' below). Next came the KAT (catalytic converter) models, introduced to capitalise on West German tax incentives offered to buyers of new cars fitted with 'clean' exhausts from January 1st, 1986. The complications of the clean-exhaust requirements demanded more sophisticated fuelling systems than had been used up to that point, and so BMW gradually discarded Bosch fuel injection in favour of Bosch Motronic engine management sys-

Cabriolet versions of the E30 were introduced in 1986 and found a waiting market

The 3 Series range was further expanded in 1987 with touring estates

From 1991 there was a Touring version of the E34 5 Series, as well

The BMW Story

095

tems. From 1989, of course, with catalytic converters obligatory throughout the EEC, all BMWs have used the Motronic system - with the exception of the diesels which rely on the diesel equivalent by Bosch, which is called DDE (Digital Diesel Electronics).

One obvious benefit of the switch to catalytic converters in Europe was that BMW no longer needed to build radically different versions of its cars for the emissions-regulated US market; and in fact the BMWs of the Eighties were designed so that they met US regulations with the very minimum of modifications. This of course reduced production costs and also created much more attractive-looking BMWs for the USA than those Seventies models spoiled by hideous extended bumpers.

The Eighties also saw BMW embracing four-valve engine technology, primarily as a way of improving top-end performance. The first four-valve BMW was the Motorsport-developed engine in the M1 supercar at the end of the Seventies. A version of that engine also appeared in the M635 CSi coupé in 1983, and then the M3 in 1986 and M5 in 1988 took on four-valve engines. Shortly after that, four-valve technology filtered down to the 'everyday' BMWs, when the 318i took on a four-valve four-cylinder engine in August 1989. Since then, there have been four-valve sixes in the 520i and 525i, and of course the new V8s originally developed for the 7 Series cars also have four valves per cylinder. It is arguable that the four-valve engines in the E34 5 Series cars lacked the refinement of earlier BMW small-block sixes, but the large-capacity V8s certainly leave no grounds whatsoever for complaint as far as refinement is concerned.

The six-cylinder diesel engines

BMW started to look at diesel power as

long ago as 1975, in the wake of the 1973-74 oil crisis. It was a fearsome challenge, and not only because there was no knowledge of compression-ignition engines at BMW. The company had established a solid reputation for the excellence of its petrol engines, and any diesel alternative which was not going to detract from the BMW image would have to be a lot more refined than anything which was around in the mid-Seventies.

Chief engine designer Karlheinz Lange decided to save time by basing the new diesel engine on the existing M60 small-block six-cylinder. By 1978, he had designed a new direct-injection cylinder head, and prototype engines were running. To get the necessary performance, he had added a turbocharger - and the result was a power output to rival any passenger car diesel then on the market. Installed in a 5 Series saloon, the engine was demonstrated to selected journalists in 1978. Unfortunately, it would be five years before it entered production, while BMW worked through an abortive alliance with Austrian diesel specialists Steyr-Daimler-Puch and built a new engine factory at Steyr. The first production M21 turbodiesel engines were not built until March 1983.

The new engine was first made available in the E28 5 Series, which was then badged as a 524td. With 115bhp from 2443cc, it had outstanding performance for a diesel, as well as a character which was wholly in keeping with the BMW image of performance and refinement. The engine attracted attention across the Atlantic, too, and Ford bought a quantity to offer in some of its Lincoln luxury models in 1984-85, just before the US diesel market collapsed.

A less powerful normally-aspirated version arrived in the 324d in 1985, and the following year found its way into the short-lived 524d. Then a 324td was made avail-

Driving Machines

The E34 was a natural home for BMW's superb second-generation diesel engine. Shown in cutaway view here is a 525tds

able with the original turbocharged engine. In 1987, the turbodiesel six was fitted with Bosch's Digital Diesel Electronics (DDE) management system to control emissions, although power and torque were unaffected.

The second-generation engine was the M51, with a longer stroke to give a flatter torque curve. This 2498cc engine was developed from the beginning to be saleable to other car makers, and has so far appeared in the Range Rover and in the Opel Omega as well as in BMW's own cars. It became available in 1991, with the same 115bhp as its predecessor or with 143bhp when intercooled.

Although diesel BMWs are rare in Britain, they sell strongly in continental Europe. BMW claims to have built 250,000 of its first-generation M21 engines, of which around 165,000 were turbocharged.

The X-cars

Just as Mercedes-Benz had felt itself under pressure from BMW in the late Seventies, so BMW began to sense Audi breathing down its neck in the early Eighties. In particular, Audi had attacked BMW on the sporting ground where it had built its reputation, by introducing the four-wheel drive Quattro coupé and than offering that car's technology in its more mundane saloons.

BMW responded by developing a permanent four-wheel drive system with a 37% front to 63% rear torque split, which it introduced during 1985 as an option in the 2.5-litre engined E30. The car was known as a 325iX, and remained the only BMW with four-wheel drive until the 525iX was introduced in 1991. Cost deterred many buyers, and neither model proved very popular despite the undoubted traction advantages of four-wheel drive.

The BMW Story

The E28 5 Series

All models were four-door saloons with a wheelbase of 103.3 inches.

model	period	cc	bhp	at rpm	cylinders/fuel system
518	1981-1984	1766	90	5500	4/Single Pierburg carburettor
518i	1984-1987	1766	105	5800	4/Bosch L-Jetronic injection
520i	1981-1985	1990	125	5800	6/Bosch K-Jetronic injection
520i	1985-1987	1990	129	6000	6/Bosch L-Jetronic fuel injection
520i KAT	1986-1987	1990	129	6000	6/Bosch Motronic management
524d	1986-1987	2443	86	4600	6/diesel; Indirect injection
524td	1983-1987	2443	115	4800	6/turbocharged diesel; Indirect injection & Garrett turbocharger
525e	1984-1987	2693	129	4800	6/Bosch Motronic management
525i	1981-1987	2494	150	5500	6/Bosch L-Jetronic fuel injection
528i	1981-1987	2788	184	5800	6/Bosch L-Jetronic fuel injection
535i and M535i	1985-1987	3430	185	5400	6/Bosch ME-Motronic engine management system
M5	1985-1987	3453	286	6500	4-valve 6/Bosch Motronic engine management system

The E30 3 Series

All models had a wheelbase of 101.2 inches except the M3 (100.8 inches). All models were available in saloon form with both two and four doors, except for the M3 (two-door only) and the 324d and 324td (four-door only).Baur targa-top cabriolets were available on the 318i, 320i, 320i KAT, 323i and 325e.Full cabriolets were available on the 318i KAT, 320i KAT, 325i, 325i KAT, 325iX, 325iX KAT and M3. Touring estates were available on the 316i KAT and 318i KAT from 1989-1995, on the 320i KAT from 1987-1995 and on all 325i and 325iX models from 1987 to 1992.

model	period	cc	bhp	at rpm	cylinders/fuel system
316	1983-1987	1766	90	5500	4/Single Pierburg carburettor
316i KAT	1987-1988	1766	102	5800	4/Bosch L-Jetronic fuel injection
316i KAT	1987-1995	1596	100	5500	4/Bosch Motronic management
318i	1983-1986	1766	105	5800	4/Bosch L-Jetronic fuel injection
318i KAT	1984-1987	1766	102	5800	4/Bosch L-Jetronic fuel injection
318i KAT	1987-1995	1796	113	5500	4/Bosch Motronic management
318iS KAT	1989-1991	1796	136	6000	4-valve 4/Bosch Motronic M1.7 engine management system
320i	1983-1986	1990	125	5800	(to August 1985)
		or	129	6000	(from September 1985) 6/Bosch L-Jetronic fuel injection
320i KAT	1986-1992	1990	129	6000	6/Bosch Motronic management

E30 continued

model	period	cc	bhp	at rpm	cylinders/fuel system
323i	1983-1985	2316	139	5300	(to August 1983)
		or	150	6000	(from September 1983)
					6/Bosch L-Jetronic fuel injection
324d	1985-1991	2443	86	4600	6/diesel; Indirect injection
324td	1987-1991	2443	115	4800	6/turbodiesel; Indirect injection and Garrett turbocharger
325e KAT	1985-1986	2693	122	4250	6/Bosch Motronic management
325i	1985-1986	2494	171	5800	6/Bosch ME-Motronic engine management system
325i KAT	1986-1992	2494	170	5800	6/Bosch ME-Motronic engine management system
325iX	1985-1986	(As contemporary 325i but with four-wheel drive)			
325iX KAT	1986-1992	(As contemporary 325i KAT but with four-wheel drive)			
M3 KAT	1986-1991	2302	195-215	6750	four-valve 4/Bosch Motronic ML engine management system

The E34 5 Series

All models were available as four-door saloons and had a wheelbase of 108.7 inches. Touring estate models were available from 1991 on the 520i, 525i, 525iX and 525tds; from 1992 on the 530i and M5; and from 1993 on the 518i and 525td.
All petrol-engined models had a Bosch Motronic engine management system.
All turbodiesel models had indirect injection and a Garrett turbocharger.

model	period	cc	bhp	at rpm	cylinders/fuel system
518i	1989-1995	1796	113	5500	4/petrol
520	1988-1990	1991	129	6000	6/petrol
520i	1990-1995	1991	150	5900	6/petrol
524td	1988-1991	2443	115	4800	6/turbodiesel
525i	1988-1990	2494	170	5800	6/petrol
525i	1990-1995	2494	192	5900	6/petrol
525iX	1991-1995	(As contemporary 525i but with four-wheel drive)			
525td	1993-1995	2498	115	4800	6/turbodiesel
525tds	1991-1995	2498	143	4800	6/intercooled turbodiesel
530i	1988-1990	2986	188	5800	6/petrol
530i	1992-1995	2997	218	5800	four-valve V8/petrol
535i	1988-1991	3430	211	5700	6/petrol
540i	1992-1995	3982	286	5800	four-valve V8/petrol
M5	1988-1991	3535	315	6900	four-valve 6/petrol
M5	1992-1995	3795	340	6900	four-valve 6/petrol

The BMW Story

Motorcycles continued to play an important part in BMW's product range. This K1100LT was ordered by a British police force

The E46, introduced in 1998, was the fourth generation of BMW's hugely successful 3 Series

Driving Machines

Chapter 12
TODAY AND TOMORROW

It's still far too early to put the first part of the Nineties into any sort of historical perspective. Nevertheless, there can be no doubting that the period has been incredibly successful for the company, which has continued to increase its market presence, continued to increase sales and - last but certainly not least - come up with some mouth-watering products which have pushed it right to the top of the worldwide motor manufacturers' heap. Even Mercedes-Benz, for so long sitting in an apparently unassailable position at the pinnacle of automotive achievement, has been forced to re-think its strategy to face the BMW challenge.

Look at it like this: in the early Nineties, BMW has established its own $600 million manufacturing plant in the USA to serve the country which has for so long been its biggest export market; it has bought Britain's Rover Group, which of course incorporates the incredibly successful Land Rover division; and it even bought Rolls-Royce after entering into an alliance with the British maker which was to see its new models powered by BMW engines. Its stunning E32 7 Series and the even more astonishing E38 which followed it have been widely acclaimed as superior to Mercedes' overweight S Class saloons; the E36 3 Series introduced in 1991 set new stan-

dards in the compact saloon class and gave way to the E46 range in 1998; and the E39 5 Series introduced in 1995 was immediately acclaimed as the finest medium-sized saloon in the world. As if that is not enough, BMW has also produced the Z1 and Z3 sports cars to broaden its range and enhance its image. Need we mention that every single recent BMW has been stunningly attractive to look at, mechanically sophisticated and durable, and has embodied the dual characteristics of practicality and sporting potential?

Looking for a drawback, we can find only one. Modern BMWs are seriously expensive pieces of machinery. Even the entry-level 3 Series will make a sizeable dent in your (or your company's) wallet, and the enormous cost of the E31 8 Series must be one of the reasons why it was not particularly successful. Then there is the question of personalising. Once the shock of the initial purchase price has worn off, owners of modern BMWs often become addicted to the purchase of bolt-on goodies. What, after all, distinguishes your 3 Series from the crowd more effectively than a new set of alloy wheels, a spoiler from one of the recognised tuning companies, some black chrome and maybe a rechip of the engine management system? But then, that is half the fun of modern BMW ownership ...

The Just 4/2 concept car of 1995 was purely a show special, which combined the best of motorcycle and open sports car

The BMW Story

Long-standing production models - the E31 8 Series and E36 3 Series

The 8 Series coupe was massively impressive, but failed to sell as well as BMW had hoped

BMW introduced new models at such a rate in the first half of the Nineties that by 1998 the oldest production model was the E31 8 Series, the flagship coupé which replaced the much-loved 6 Series cars in 1989.

The 8 Series bristled with the latest in BMW technology, from traction control and four-wheel steering to adaptive suspension and intelligent automatic transmission. The first cars, which wore 850i badges, had the 300bhp V12 engine from the 7 Series saloon. From 1992, however, the original car was renamed an 850Ci and was joined by a 380bhp 850CSi with a 5576cc version of the V12. A year later, the two V12s were joined by an 840Ci, with the 286bhp 4-litre V8 engine.

The 8 Series has always been rather controversial, not least because of its high price. This made it inaccessible to many people, who then felt justified in criticising it. Some people argued that its ride comfort is poor, although few people who had actually driven one would argue with the overall excellence of even the entry-level 840Ci.

Right at the other end of the BMW range was the E36 3 Series, introduced in saloon form in 1990. The range was expanded consistently since then, to embrace a coupé (from 1992), a two-door cabriolet (from 1993), a two-door Compact (from 1994) and a touring estate (from 1995). In Germany, Baur also made a four-door

The E36 models brought the 3 Series into the 1990s

Driving Machines

With the arrival of the Compact in 1994, the E36 range took on the best of the hot hatchbacks, as well as the small saloons

cabriolet, which was introduced in 1992. Engines ran the full gamut from the entry-level 1.6-litre four-cylinder through to the 2.8-litre six-cylinder, plus of course a 3-litre six in the M3 models and the four-cylinder and six-cylinder turbocharged diesels.

The E36 was of course the third-generation 3 Series, and was undoubtedly the most successful to date. Build quality and driving dynamics were first-rate (although the Compacts had a less refined rear suspension than the other models), and the car was far and away the most attractively styled in its class. With an enormous range of options, the E36 really did offer something for everyone. Nevertheless, the fourth-generation E46 models which were announced during 1998 promised to improve on its few shortcomings.

New kids on the block - the E38 7 Series, E39 5 Series and E46 3 Series

The curvaceous styling of 1990's E36 3 Series set a pattern which other BMWs of the early Nineties would follow. First to come was the new 7 Series, or E38, which was announced in 1994. That was followed by the fourth-generation 5 Series, or E39, in 1995.

The sleek and sporty demeanour of the

E38 was conditioned to a large extent by the negative reactions to Mercedes' bloated-looking S Class. BMW was determined not to make the same mistake, and to some eyes went too far in the other direction. Nevertheless, the E38 was an astonishingly competent blend of high technology, svelte styling and luxury appointments with the handling and performance of a sports saloon half its size. The V8-engined 730i and 740i were accompanied from the beginning by a V12-powered 750i (there were long-wheelbase 740s and 750s, too), and from 1995 a 728i brought the entry-level price down to almost reasonable levels. All models of the 7 Series range represent incredible value for money when compared with their natural rivals.

The E39 range arrived in saloon form only, with 2-litre, 2.3-litre and 2.8-litre six-cylinder petrol engines, a 2.5-litre six-cylinder diesel, and 3.5-litre and 4.4-litre petrol V8s. Touring estates were announced in 1996, and the range-topping M5 in 1998. When *BMW Car* magazine drove one of the first 528i saloons across Europe, it described it as 'the most complete, sophisticated saloon in the world - at any price.' Few people would disagree with that sentiment.

The fourth-generation 3 Series was announced during 1998. While its styling was evolutionary rather than revolutionary, it was instantly recognisable by its new

The BMW Story

'face', featuring clear covers over the headlamps, accentuated by concave lower mouldings. The car featured aluminium suspension components, as seen on the E39 5 Series, and was laden with electronic traction and driving aids. A stiffer bodyshell on a longer wheelbase and wider track also brought more interior space - long-overdue in the 3 Series range.

The E46 also brought new engines, in the shape of a four-cylinder turbodiesel with common-rail injection and a balancer-shaft petrol four-cylinder. The twin-cam six-cylinders meanwhile took on 'double VANOS', with variable valve timing for both inlet and exhaust camshafts.

Once again, production overlapped with that of the outgoing E36 models. Coupé, convertible, touring and Compact versions of the old car remained available after the introduction of the E46 as a four-door saloon.

Top the E38 7 Series range was the V12-powered long-wheelbase 750iL

The X5

The boom in sport-utility vehicles which had begun in the 1980s had largely passed BMW by, but persistent demand from the USA led the company to develop a stylish 4x4 of its own. Announced in 1998 for 1999 availability, the X5 was designed to bring all the BMW driving dynamics to the sport-utility market, previously dominated by large and rather ponderous machines. To emphasise that this was something different, BMW coined a new description for it: they called the X5 a Sport Activity Vehicle.

The 1999 X5 was BMW's first entry into the Sport Utility Vehicle sector

Driving Machines

The V8 and V12 engines

Why did BMW switch to vee engines for its flagship saloons and coupés when its reputation for silky in-line sixes was second to none? Part of the reason was to tackle Jaguar (with a V12 in its big saloons) and Mercedes-Benz (whose latest S Class has a big V12 and several V8s), but it was also clear that extra performance with the necessary refinement could only be achieved by capacity increases. There is only so far a six-cylinder engine can go without becoming long and unwieldy, whereas a V12 or V8 can have a much greater swept volume within a relatively compact length. So when BMW wanted a 300bhp 5-litre for the 7 Series in 1987, a V12 was the obvious choice.

Four-valve technology and sophisticated management systems of course make these large-capacity engines remarkably fuel-efficient, and there is no doubt that vee engines are here to stay at the top of the BMW range. The latest addition is a 3.9-litre V8 turbodiesel, intended for the 7 Series luxury saloons and undoubtedly destined to set new standards for compression-ignition engines in cars.

The E32 7 Series cars were the first to have the V12 engine

The trend towards vee engine configurations continued with the announcement of a turbodiesel V8

The BMW Story

Alternative fuels

Ever since the early Seventies, BMW has been working hard on alternative fuels for its cars. The ever-tightening US emissions laws and the spiralling increases in the price of petrol after the two oil crises of the Seventies were the main reasons why the company devoted so much effort to this research.

The introduction of diesel engines in the early Eighties was the first step in BMW's alternative fuel strategy. But diesel is another 'traditional' fuel for cars, and its main value is that the diesel combustion process is much more energy-efficient than the petrol one. The combination of this with significantly cheaper diesel prices (in many countries) makes the diesel-powered car an attractive short-term solution. Unfortunately, diesel will run out at the same time as petrol: they both come from oil.

Spurred on by American calls for the zero-emissions vehicle and by the Californian demand for a proportion of new cars sold in that state to meet ultra-low-emissions standards by 1998 (a demand since relaxed), BMW set about developing electric vehicles. The first battery-powered BMWs were in fact built in 1972, and were a pair of converted 1602 saloons used at that year's Olympic Games in Munich. However, it was not until the announcement of the E1 prototype in 1991 that the company had a really viable electric car to show. A modified E2 version appeared at the Los Angeles Show in January 1992, but thereafter BMW turned to hybrid vehicles. The second-generation E1 prototype of 1993 combined a 45bhp electric motor with an 82bhp four-cylinder petrol engine (from the K1000 motorcycle) and could be driven by either engine.

The main thrust of BMW's alternative-fuel research since 1979, however, has been to develop a car which will run on hydrogen. As hydrogen comes from water, and water is an infinitely renewable resource, this is clearly the most promising option. A staged series of developments towards the hydrogen-powered BMW reached an important point at the end of 1995, when the first BMWs powered by natural gas were announced: in Germany, you can now buy a 316g Compact and a 518g touring, both driven by this alternative fuel. The next stage in the development programme will be cars powered by liquefied natural gas, and the third and final development will be the hydrogen-powered car. BMW hopes to have such vehicles ready early in the next century. Will we then be able to fill up our new 7 Series from a hosepipe linked to the domestic water supply?

The second-generation E1 electric car was actually a hybrid, with a petrol engine as well as electric power

Driving Machines

The Z-cars

BMW's Z1 Roadster was developed in such secrecy that many people working for the company believed it was no more than a design study. But no - it was proudly presented on the BMW stand at the 1987 Frankfurt Motor Show and limited production began in time for the first deliveries to be made in March 1989.

BMW had by then taken orders for 5000 cars, which looked extremely promising for the Z1's future. Unfortunately, this was boom time in the West, and a large number of those orders had been placed by speculators. Before long, the market was flooded with one-owner, barely-used Z1s at inflated prices. It was during 1990 that the first signs of the recession became apparent; demand for the Z1 fell and BMW was forced to increase its showroom price by a hefty 10%. By the end of the year, dealers had to offer substantial discounts to shift the Z1s in their showrooms. BMW decided to cut and run - and Z1 production ceased in June 1991 after just 8000 cars had been built.

The second of BMW's Z-cars was not actually called the Z2 but the Z13. This time, it was a prototype rather than a production model, a concept vehicle which explored the possibilities of the ultra-compact, energy-efficient car. Unveiled at the Geneva Motor Show in March 1993, the Z13 was a three-seater saloon just 134 inches long and sitting on a 90.5-inch wheelbase. Power came from an 82bhp motorcycle engine of 1100cc which gave 0-62mph in 10 seconds, a maximum of 112mph, and fuel economy of about 55mpg. To prove that vital ingredients need not be omitted, the little car had both ABS and airbags. The Z13 has so far remained a feasibility study, although BMW claimed it could be in production by 1998. It might well be, too, if the company feels obliged to match Mercedes' forthcoming A-class small car.

The third Z-car was the Z3 Roadster, ultimately a more practical machine than the Z1 but no less good-looking and with a deliberately nostalgic flavour to its styling. Powered initially by either 1.8-litre or 1.9-litre engines, it entered production at BMW's new factory in Spartanburg, South Carolina during 1995. More recently, the range has been developed to include a 2.8-litre six-cylinder option, and the fabulous M roadster and M coupé, both prepared by the M (née Motorsport) Division.

The latest addition to the Z range is a fabulous supercar called the Z8. Based on a concept-car called the Z-07, which picked up styling elements of the 507 roadster from the 1950s, this open two-seater is powered by the M5's 400bhp Motorsport V8 engine.

Built in America: the BMW Z3 roadster

First of the Z-cars was the exotic Z1

The BMW Story

BMW motorcycles, 1986-1996

Innovative technology saw BMW keep ahead of its rivals in the motorcycle field between 1986 and 1996. New engines included a three-cylinder for the K Series in 1986, and a four-valve version of the four-cylinder motor on a super-sports edition of the K100 called the K1 which was announced in 1989. Then 1994 saw the arrival of a Bombardier-Rotax-built single for the Italian-assembled F650 Funduro trail bike which - horror of horrors! - actually employed chain-drive to the rear wheel.

New suspensions came in, too. What BMW called the Paralever rear suspension gave better wheel control by adding joints and links to the swinging arm in 1988, while the 1993 Telelever was a radically new concept in front suspension. ABS has been available on some models since 1988; some bikes have catalytic converters while others have less elaborate emissions-control systems; and BMW has dipped into the retro-look market with a 1986 revival of the R100RS twin and with a number of subsequent models.

Cruising in BMW style: the R1200C

C1 commuter bike, launched in 2000

*Even the F650 Funduro was
a new departure for BMW*

Driving Machines

BRIEF SPECIFICATIONS

Note: Specifications are provided for only those model-ranges which are now complete.

The E32 7 Series

All models were four-door saloons with a wheelbase of 111.5 inches (standard cars) or 116 inches (long-wheelbase types).
All engines had Bosch Motronic management systems.

model	period	cc	bhp	at rpm	engine type
730i	1986-1992	2986	188	5800	6-cylinder
730i	1992-1994	2997	218	5800	V8-cylinder
735i	1986-1992	3430	211	5700	6-cylinder
735iL	1986-1992	3430	211	5700	6-cylinder
740i	1992-1994	3982	286	5800	V8-cylinder
740iL	1992-1994	3982	286	5800	V8-cylinder
750i	1987-1994	4988	300	5200	V12-cylinder
750iL	1987-1994	4988	300	5200	V12-cylinder

The Z1 Roadster

All models were two-seater roadsters with a wheelbase of 96.5 inches.

model	period	cc	bhp	at rpm	engine type
Z1	1988-1991	2494	170	5800	6-cylinder; Bosch Motronic

The E36 3 Series

There were four-door saloon, two-door coupé, two-door Compact, touring estate and two-door convertible models, all on a 106.2-inch wheelbase. Not every engine was available with every body style; the M3, for example, came only as a Coupé or a Convertible. All petrol engines had Bosch Motronic management systems, and all diesels had Bosch DDE management systems.

model	period	cc	bhp	at rpm	engine type
316i	1990 on	1596	102	5500	4-cylinder
318i	1990 on	1796	113	5500	4-cylinder
318iS	1992 on	1796	140	6000	four-valve 4-cylinder
318tds	1995 on	1665	90	4400	4-cylinder intercooled turbodiesel
318ti	1994 on	1895	140	6000	four-valve 4-cylinder
320i	1990 on	1991	150	5900	four-valve 6-cylinder
323i	1996 on	2494	170	5500	four-valve 6-cylinder
325i	1990 on	2494	192	6000	four-valve 6-cylinder
325td	1991 on	2498	115	4800	6-cylinder turbodiesel
325tds	1993 on	2498	143	4800	6-cylinder intercooled turbodiesel
328i	1995 on	2793	193	5300	four-valve 6-cylinder
M3	1992 on	2990	286	7000	four-valve 6-cylinder
M3 Evo	1996 on	3201	321	7400	four-valve 6-cylinder

The BMW Story

BMW's clover-leaf shaped Headquarters building and the BMW Museum, in Munich

Driving Machines

Appendix A
THE BMW GROUP

The BMW Group is a large industrial combine with interests in many fields besides BMW cars. This Appendix provides an overview of the Group as it stood at the end of the Nineties.

Who owns BMW, and who runs it?

BMW has been owned for many years by the rather secretive Quandt family, who had built up large business empires in the Fifties. The brothers Herbert and Harald Quandt bought up large quantities of BMW shares and rescued the company in 1960 when it was going through its worst period. Harald Quandt died in 1969, but since then the family has maintained its controlling interest in the BMW Group.

BMW is run by two Boards. The Supervisory Board regularly reviews the company's business strategies, keeps an eye on its financial progress, and makes new appointments to the Board of Management. Its Chairman in 2000 was still Eberhard von Kuenheim. The Board of Management consists primarily of senior individuals with direct responsibility for engineering in various areas of the company. Joachim Milberg became its Chairman in 1999.

BMW Cars

Car manufacture may be BMW's core activity, but it is not by any means confined to the company's German base. Although BMW makes cars or car components at six different factories in Germany, it also has factories or assembly operations in a number of overseas countries. Notable among these are the long-established factory at Rosslyn in South Africa and the recently-opened plant at Spartanburg in the USA.

Not all the BMW factories in Germany build complete cars. Tools and pressings come from Eisenach (a new factory opened recently in BMW's traditional home town),

plastic parts and light metal castings and components come from Landshut, and both petrol and diesel engines come from Steyr (actually just across the border in neighbouring Austria). Both body shells for convertibles and sundry other parts have been produced at Wackersdorf since 1990, where BMW is now building an industrial park to accommodate its suppliers of systems and parts. Seats and instrument panels are already coming from Wackersdorf, which will later also take over the supply of German-made parts to the South African and US factories.

Complete cars come from Munich and Regensburg, which both build 3 Series models, and from Dingolfing, where 5 Series and 7 Series are made. The Rosslyn plant in South Africa also builds complete 3 Series cars, while the Spartanburg plant in the USA makes the Z3 range and X5; in each case, some components are shipped out from Germany. In addition, 3 Series KD kits for overseas assembly are made at Munich, while Dingolfing puts together the KD kits for other models assembled overseas. The kit-assembly operations outside Germany are at Toluca in Mexico, where the plant is owned by BMW, and in five countries in the Asian-Pacific region where the assembly plants are run by locally-owned companies.

BMW built 639,400 cars worldwide in 1996 - an all-time record for the company. Of these, more than 50,000 were made in the USA and some 15,000 in South Africa.

The concept of a network of linked factories is echoed by BMW's network of linked research and development centres. The primary R&D centre for cars is in Munich, but diesel engine development is carried out at Steyr and there is a styling centre (more trendily but rather misleadingly known as a design centre) in California, known as Charles W. Pelly Designworks Inc.

In addition, BMW is able to call on the Rover Group's Design and Engineering Centre at Gaydon in Warwickshire.

BMW aero engines

BMW started as an aircraft engine manufacturer back in 1916, and when cars came upon the scene in 1928, the aero engine business became the Aircraft Engine Division of BMW. In 1934 it was set up as a separate company called BMW Flugmotorenbau GmbH, and it went on to put one of the world's first jet engines on test in 1943, and to have it in production a year later. However, a three-year ban on production of all kinds was BMW's punishment from the Allies at the end of the war for making Hitler's rockets, and aero engine production stopped altogether.

It started again in 1955, when a new company called BMW Triebwerkbau GmbH was set up at Allach, near Munich. West Germany was to have her own military forces again from 1956, and the new Air Force was going to need aero engines. However, the new company lasted just 10 years before being sold in 1965, and there was then a period of 25 years in which BMW did not make any aero engines.

That all changed again in 1990, when BMW got together with the aero engine division of Rolls-Royce and established BMW Rolls-Royce GmbH at Dahlewitz, near Berlin, for the joint development of a new range of engines. The BR700 range of engines offered class-leading standards of power, fuel economy and environmental friendliness. First into production (in 1996) was the BR710, intended for the large executive jets made by Gulfstream and Bombardier and for the eventual refit of the Royal Navy's Nimrod reconnaissance aircraft at the beginning of the next century. Next was expected to be the more powerful BR715, intended for the new

McDonnel Douglas MD-95-30 regional jet liner. In addition, BMW Rolls-Royce has developed the RE220 auxiliary power unit for aircraft (which runs their electrical systems independently of the main engines when they are on the ground) in conjunction with Allied Signal.

So far, however, the aero engine division hasn't proved to be one of BMW's more profitable ventures. During 1997, rumours abounded that the Group was looking at its future very closely indeed.

The Rover Group

When BMW bought the Rover Group in January 1994, there wasn't much doubt that its main objective was to get its hands on Land Rover. After all, Land Rover was a world leader in four-wheel drives, the four-wheel drive boom seemed set to continue, and BMW didn't have any entry in the four-wheel drive market.

However, under British Aerospace, the last owners of what in the bad old Seventies had been known as British Leyland, the separate car and Land Rover sides of Rover had been carefully integrated so that a split in any future sell-off would have been out of the question. So BMW got Rover Cars as well.

The new Rover models which have appeared since the BMW takeover had all been under development before 1994, so BMW's influence on them ranged from nil to extremely minimal. But the first new project which BMW approved in 1994 was the Land Rover Freelander, the new model introduced at the 1998 Frankfurt Show. There was no BMW influence on the car's engineering, but BMW did inject capital to give the new factory where the car will be built even higher standards than the Land Rover engineers had hoped for.

Driving Machines

In the future, expect BMW influence on Rover Cars products (shared engines, drivetrains, etc) and Land Rover influence is evident on BMW's X5 luxury off-roader.

The Motorcycle division

BMW's motorcycle division was established in 1923, when the company was looking for new business opportunities. That year, the R23 model was introduced at the Paris Show, with three features which would become BMW hallmarks - a flat-twin engine set across the frame, unit construction with the gearbox bolted to the back of the engine, and shaft drive to the rear wheel.

Motorcycle manufacture was transferred from Munich to Eisenau early in the 1939-1945 war; the Eisenau factory fell into Soviet Russian hands in 1945 and was irretrievably lost. BMW got back into business slowly with a new single-cylinder model in 1948 and has been building motorcycles successfully ever since. For a period of 20 years, starting in 1954, BMW products held the World Sidecar Championship.

There was a slump in the motorcycle market at the end of the Sixties, but in 1969 BMW moved its factory to Berlin and announced the first of a remarkable new product range, featuring a patented Compact Drive System with a water-cooled four-cylinder engine, shaft drive and single swinging arm. In 1980, a BMW motorcycle took the first of five wins in the tough Paris-Dakar Rally.

Currently, BMW makes about 40,000 motor cycles a year at its Berlin plant, a new one opened in 1983. In addition, some 8500 F Series (Funduro) BMW bikes are built by Aprilia at Noale near Venice. Assembly of BMW motorcycles has just begun in Indonesia for local markets.

What is planned for the future?

BMW plans to improve the links among its various manufacturing sites, and we can expect to see far more overseas manufacture - not least because high labour rates in Germany and a strong Deutschmark make German-built cars and components expensive by global standards.

We can also expect to see stronger BMW links with its Rover Group subsidiary, as car components are shared and design and engineering expertise is moved around between the two car companies. However, there's no need to fear that this cross-fertilisation will dilute the BMW marque in any way - or the Rover one, for that matter. Current plans are to keep the two as distinctive as possible.

We can expect some interesting engine developments, too. BMW has started work on a new engine factory at Hams Hall, near Birmingham in the UK, which will build four-cylinder engines in the 1.6-litre to 2-litre size range. These engines will be shared by BMW and Rover cars. In addition, a new agreement signed with Chrysler in the USA envisages the joint development of smaller (1.4-litre to 1.6-litre) four-cylinder engines, based on a Chrysler design. Among these will be the engine which will power Rover's next-generation Mini. The 1998 merger of Chrysler with BMW's traditional rivals in the car world, Daimler-Benz, does not appear to have affected these plans.

The other BMW Group companies

Some companies in the BMW Group have been established purely to support the Group's core activities. These include BMW Finance and BMW Insurance. The finance company organises loan and leasing financing to assist customers in the purchase of BMW products, and has branches in 15

The BMW Story

countries. Some 70% of its business, however, is carried out in Germany and the USA. The insurance company has been operating since 1970 and arranges insurance on behalf of the finance company for buyers of BMW cars and motorcycles.

Other companies were established initially to support the Group's core activities, but have since gone on to operate in the wider marketplace. BETEK is a 160-strong construction company, consisting mostly of architects and engineers, which co-ordinates building work at BMW's own sites. It is currently working on projects at Wackersdorf and Regensburg. However, BETEK has also co-ordinated major projects for outside clients, such as the construction of the new buildings at the Munich Technical University in Garching.

Softlab GmbH is a Munich-based computer software company which was established some 25 years ago. It advises large corporate clients - many of them in the car industry - on the best products to use to meet their requirements. Softlab currently has some 900 employees worldwide, with subsidiaries in Europe, Japan and the USA. Then there is Kontron Elektronik GmbH, with 400 employees worldwide engaged in the development and sale of computer-assisted products and services for industry and research. Current products include portable and static industrial computers, programmes and equipment for image and material analysis, and digital cameras and digitisers used in CAD and computer-aided construction.

And let us not forget ...

... that BMW also conducts research into transport systems as a whole, in order to keep itself in the forefront of developments and ensure itself a place in whatever transport systems may come to take over from the car in the future.

Evidence of the company's work is already visible in the COMPANION project to develop a roadside warning and information system, a kind of 'intelligent road' which uses light signals from roadside beacons to warn drivers of traffic hold-ups, roadworks or fog ahead. A test installation of COMPANION is already functioning on some 9km of motorway near Munich airport, in a joint venture between BMW and the State of Bavaria.

Driving Machines

Appendix B
BMW'S E-SERIES CODES

Since the mid-1960s, all mainstream BMWs have had a factory type code beginning with E (non-mainstream models have had Z codes). This E stands for Entwicklung (development) and is allocated at the design stage; the numerical order therefore relates to the date when design commenced, and not to the date when a model entered production. Not every project has made it past the design stage, and there are therefore many gaps in the sequence of numbers associated with the production BMWs. The E1 and E2 electric cars are not included in this list, because the E in their designations stands for Electric and they do not belong to the same design numbering sequence as the mainstream models.

E3	2500, 2800 and subsequent big saloons of this range, 1968-1977.
E6	Facelifted '02 models, 1973-1975. (The original '02s did not have an E code).
E9	Six-cylinder coupés from 2500CS to 3.0 CSL, 1968-1971.
E10	2002 turbo, variant of the E6 '02 models, 1973-1975.
E12	First-generation 5 Series saloons, 1972-1981.
E21	First-generation 3 Series, 1975-1982.
E23	First-generation 7 Series saloons, 1977-1986.
E24	6 Series coupés, 1976-1989.
E26	M1 mid-engined supercar, 1978-1980.
E28	Second-generation 5 Series, 1981-1988.
E30	Second-generation 3 Series, 1983-1991.
E31	8 Series coupés, 1989 on.
E32	Second-generation 7 Series, 1986-1994.
E34	Third-generation 5 Series saloons, 1988-1996.
E36	Third-generation 3 Series, 1991 on.
E38	Third-generation 7 Series, 1994 on.
E39	Fourth generation 5 Series saloons, 1995 on.
E46	Fourth-generation 3 Series, 1997 on.
E53	X5 sport-activity vehicle, 2000 on.

The BMW Story

The M60 V8 engines were announced in April 1992

Driving Machines

Appendix C
BMW ENGINES SINCE 1961: A CONCORDANCE

In 1961, BMW announced the first of the powerplants which gave the company the reputation it has today. Since then, the evolution of the engine ranges has been extremely complicated. This concordance is intended to make the picture a little clearer. Note that there are two different engines with the M60 design code.

M10	Four-cylinders, 1961 on.
M20	Small-block six-cylinders, 1985 on.
M21	Diesel and turbodiesel six-cylinders, 1985 on.
M30	Big-block six-cylinders, 1968 on.
M40	Four-cylinders, 1987 on.
M41	Turbodiesel four-cylinders, 1994 on.
M42	Four-valve four-cylinders, 1986 on.
M43	Four-cylinders, 1993 on.
M44	Four-valve four-cylinders, 1994 on.
M47	Turbodiesel four-cylinders, 1998 on.
M50	VANOS four-valve six-cylinders with iron blocks, 1992 on.
M51	Turbodiesel six-cylinders, 1991 on.
M52	VANOS four-valve six-cylinders with alloy blocks, 1995 on.
M57	Turbodiesel six-cylinders, 1998 on.
M60	Small-block six-cylinders, 1977 on.
M60	V8s, 1992 on.
M62	V8s, 1996 on.
M70	V12s, 1987 on.
M73	V12s, 1995 on.
M88	Four-valve, big-block six-cylinders, 1979 on.

The BMW Story

FOUR-CYLINDER PETROL ENGINES

The M10 family, 1961-1987

Before this engine appeared in the Neue Klasse 1500 saloon (announced in 1961, into production in 1962), BMW's post-war engines had been the revived pre-war 2-litre six, an excellent but costly alloy V8, and a variety of adapted motorcycle powerplants. The M10 engine actually had its origins in a 1958 proposal by Alex von Falkenhausen for a 1-litre OHC four-cylinder intended for the BMW 700. That engine was never built, but its basic design concept was developed into the engine of the Neue Klasse. It was an oversquare design with a cast-iron block and an alloy head, and was designed with the stretchability of which BMW made full use over a period of nearly a quarter of a century.

Capacity	Bore x Stroke	Introduced	Used in
1499cc	82mm x 71mm	1961	1500
1573cc	84mm x 71mm	1964	1600, 1600TI, 1600-2, 1602, 1502, 1600GT E21 316, 315
1773cc	84mm x 80mm	1963	1800, 1800TI, 1800TI/SA
1766cc	89mm x 71mm	1968	1800, 1802 E21 316, 318, 318i, E28 518, 518i E30 316, 318i
1990cc	89mm x 80mm	1965	2000, 2002, 2002ti, 2002tii, 2000C, 2000CS E21 320, 320I, E12 520i

The 1990cc version was also developed into a turbocharged engine for the 2002 turbo in 1973, retaining the same basic layout and the same cylinder capacity.

These four-cylinder engines were always installed with a sideways tilt to allow for a low bonnet-line, and BMW planned to make use of this feature in 1969, when the company started work on a V8 which was essentially two four-cylinders on a common crankshaft. Four different capacities of the M36 engine were considered, of 3.6, 4.0. 4.5 and 5.0 litres, and some prototypes were built. However, the engine was abandoned in 1972 as too costly.

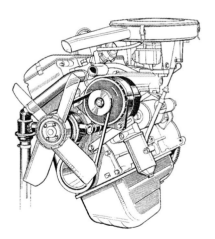

The M10 engines were installed with a 30-degree slant

The S14 engine 1986 to 1991
Based on a similar block to the M10, the S14 was only found in the E30 M3.

Capacity	Bore x Stroke	Introduced	Used in
2302cc	93.4mm x 84mm	1986	E30 M3
2467cc	95mm x 87mm	1989	E30 M3 Sport Evolution

The M40, M42, M43 and M44 engines, 1987 to date

The M40 family was drawn up as a new engine for the E30 3 Series cars. It followed the familiar BMW layout of iron block and alloy head, but the single overhead camshaft acted on hydraulic tappets and was now belt-driven instead of chain-driven. The later M43 derivative of the basic design reverted to a chain-driven overhead camshaft, as did the four-valve, twin-overhead camshaft derivatives. The two-valve M40 engines are:

Capacity	Bore x Stroke	Introduced	Used in
1596cc	84mm x 72mm	1987	E30 316i
			E36 316i
1796cc	84mm x 81mm	1987	E30 318i, 318iS
			E34 518i
			E36 318i

and the M43 derivatives (with chain-driven camshaft, engine management modifications and reduced internal friction) are as follows. Note that the 1895cc engine for the E46 also has twin balancer shafts.

Capacity	Bore x Stroke	Introduced	Used in
1596cc	84mm x 72mm	1993	E36 316i
1796cc	84mm x 81mm	1993	E36 318i
			E34 518i
1895cc	83.5mm x 85mm	1998	E46 318i

The four-valve M42 engines is:

Capacity	Bore x Stroke	Introduced	Used in
1796cc	84mm x 81mm	1989	E30 318iS

and the four-valve M44 engine is:

Capacity	Bore x Stroke	Introduced	Used in
1895cc	85mm x 83.5mm	1994	Z3, E36 318ti
			E36 318iS

The four-valve S14 engine of the original E30 M3

The BMW Story

The M30 Big-Block Sixes, 1968 to date

BMW hired Bernhard Osswald from Ford to oversee the development of its second family of new engines in the Sixties. This time, they were six-cylinder types with seven main bearings, intended to power the new E3 big saloons introduced in 1968. The successful formula of a chain-driven overhead camshaft, oversquare cylinder dimensions, and a cast-iron block with an alloy cylinder head was employed once again. Later developments (after 1972) were overseen by Gustav Ederer, and the M30 also formed the basis of the M88 four-valve engines.

Capacity	Bore x Stroke	Introduced	Used in
2494cc	86mm x 71.6mm	1968	2500, 2.5CS E12 525
2788cc	86mm x 80mm	1968	2800, 2.8L, 2800CS E12 528, 528i E23 728i E24 628CSi E28 528i
2985cc	89mm x 80mm	1971	3.0S, 3.0L, 3.0Si, 3.0CS, 3.0CSL, 3.0CSi E23 730 E32 730i E24 630CS E34 530i
3003cc	89.25mm x 80mm	1972	3.0CSi
3153cc	89.25mm x 84mm	1973	3.0CSL
3210cc	89mm x 86mm	1976	3.3Li E24 633CSi E23 733i, 732i
3295cc	89mm x 88.4mm	1974	3.3L
3430cc	92mm x 86mm	1982	E28 535i, M535i E24 635CSi E23 735i E32 735i E34 535i
3453cc	93.4mm x 84mm	1978	E12 M535i E24 635CSi E23 735i

Driving Machines

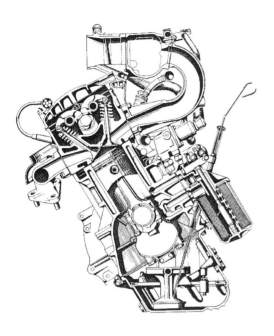

Cutaway of the 3453cc two-valve engine

The M88 was a four-valve Motorsport derivative of the M30

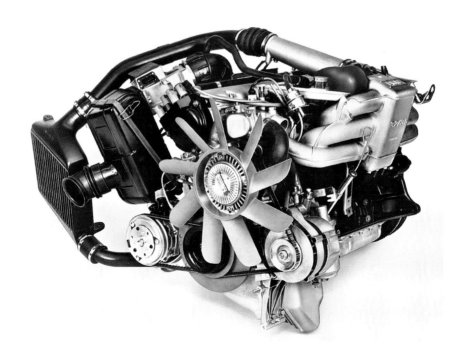

The turbocharged 745i engine was designated M102

The BMW Story

The turbocharged Big-Block Sixes, 1980-1986

The Big-Block Six was also turbocharged for use in the 745i saloons. There were two different versions, which were both redesignated as M102 engines.

Capacity	Bore x Stroke	Introduced	Used in
3210cc	89mm x 86mm	1980	745i
3430cc	92mm x 86mm	1982	745i

The M88 24-valve Six, 1979

The M30 Big-Block Six was redeveloped with twin overhead camshafts and four valves per cylinder for high-performance machinery in the late Seventies. In mid-mounted form for the M1 supercar, it was called an M88; in front-engined form for the M635CSi it was initially known as M88/3, but later recoded with the Motorsport designation S38 B35. Bore and stroke dimensions were the same as those for the 3.5-litre single overhead camshaft engine.

Capacity	Bore x Stroke	Introduced	Used in
3453cc	93.4mm x 84mm	1979	E26 M1
			E24 M635CSi
			E28 M5
3535cc	93.4mm x 86mm	1988	E34 M5
3795cc	94.6mm x 90mm	1992	E34 M5

The M60 Small-Block Sixes, 1977-1985

Many buyers of the four-cylinder BMWs wanted more performance from their cars, and some also wanted the refinement of six cylinders instead of four. The M30 six-cylinder engines were too large to fit easily into the engine bay of the forthcoming 3 Series, so work began in 1971 on a physically smaller and much lighter six-cylinder engine, which had the project code M60. It finally appeared in 1977. Once again it was an oversquare design with a single overhead camshaft and an alloy head on a cast-iron block. The crankshaft ran in seven main bearings and was made of cast iron rather than the forged steel of the M30's crankshaft, and the camshaft was driven by a toothed belt instead of a roller chain.

Capacity	Bore x Stroke	Introduced	Used in
1991cc	80mm x 66mm	1977	E21 320
			E30 320i E12 520
			E28 520i
2315cc	80mm x 76.8mm	1978	E21 323i E30 323i

The M20 small-block sixes, 1985-1993

The M60 was further developed into the M20 in the early Eighties, retaining the same bore and stroke in its 2-litre and 2.3-litre forms, which were joined by a new 2.5-litre derivative. The fuel-efficient 'eta' engine was also an M20, although it had four main bearings (to reduce internal friction losses) instead of the seven of the other M20s.

Capacity	Bore x Stroke	Introduced	Used in
1991cc	80mm x 66mm	1983	E30 320i, E34 520i E36 320i
2315cc	80mm x 76.8mm	1983	E30 323i
2494cc	84mm x 75mm	1985	E30 325i, 325iX E28 525i E34 525i, 525iX Z1, E36 325i
2693cc	84mm x 81mm	1984	E30 325e E28 525e

The M50 iron-block and VANOS sixes, 1990-1995

The next development added twin camshafts and four valves per cylinder. From 1992, the M50 had VANOS, an ingenious variable valve-timing arrangement. The M50s had cast-iron cylinder blocks and alloy heads, with chain-driven camshafts. The Motorsport-developed M3 version was called the S50 B30 while the Evo engine, the S50 B32 was the first to have a double-VANOS system, operating on both inlet and exhaust camshafts.

Capacity	Bore x Stroke	Introduced	Used in
1991cc	80mm x 66mm	1990	E34 520i, E36 320i
2494cc	84mm x 75mm	1990	E34 525i, E36 325i
2990cc	86mm x 85.8mm	1990	E36 M3
3201cc	91mm x 86mm	1996	E36 M3 Evo

The M52 VANOS all-alloy sixes, 1995 on

The M50 small-block six was redeveloped with an alloy cylinder block and was announced in 1995 in three different capacities of 2 litres, 2.5 litres and 2.8 litres. VANOS variable valve timing was once again fitted. Double-VANOS was introduced on the 2.5-litre and 2.8-litre engines for the E46 models from 1998 and .

Capacity	Bore x Stroke	Introduced	Used in
1991cc	80mm x 66mm	1995	E36 320i, E39 520i
2495cc	84mm x 75mm	1995	E36 323i, E39 523i E46 323i, E39 523i
2793cc	84mm x 84mm	1995	E36 328i, E38 728i E39 528i, Z3 2.8 E46 328i, E38 728i E39 528i, Z3 2.8

The BMW Story

V8 PETROL ENGINES

The M60 V8 engines, 1992-1996

After a gap of nearly three decades, in which it had planned to introduce new V8 engines at least once, BMW finally came up with a production V8 design for the 5 Series, 7 Series and 8 Series ranges. These all-alloy engines have four camshafts (two for each bank of cylinders) and four valves per cylinder. (And yes, they do share their design code with the early small-block six-cylinders!)

Capacity	Bore x Stroke	Introduced	Used in
2997cc	84mm x 67.6mm	1992	E34 530i
			E32 730i
3982cc	89mm x 80mm	1992	E34 540i
			E32 740i, 740iL
			E31 840i

The M62 V8 engines, 1996 to date

Redevelopment of the M60 V8s to give larger swept volumes in the mid-Nineties produced two new engines with the M62 type code. The M62 engines were equipped with VANOS variable valve timing during the 1999 model-year.

Capacity	Bore x Stroke	Introduced	Used in
3498cc	84mm x 78.9mm	1996	E38 735i
			E39 535i
4398cc	92mm x 82.7mm	1996	E38 740i
			E39 540i

From 1998, a 350bhp, twin-turbocharged version of the M62 4.4-litre V8 was supplied to Bentley Motors for use in the Arnage saloon.

The Motorsport V8 engine, 1998 to date

Developed for the E39 M5, the Motorsport version of the V8 engine carries the type-code of S62. It uses VANOS variable valve timing on all four camshafts.

Capacity	Bore x Stroke	Introduced	Used in
4941cc	94mm x 89mm	1998	E39 M5

Driving Machines

V12 PETROL ENGINES

The M70 V12 engines, 1987-1995

After threatening in the mid-Seventies to build a V12 engine which was subsequently cancelled in favour of the turbocharged sixes, BMW beat Mercedes to the punch with a V12 for its flagship 7 Series saloons a decade later. The engine had twin overhead camshafts (one on each cylinder bank) and two valves per cylinder. Note that the cylinder dimensions of the 5-litre version were identical to those of the 2.5-litre M60 Small Six. The 5.6-litre V12 developed by the Motorsport division is more correctly known as an S70 B56 engine, but is of course a derivative of the M70.

Capacity	Bore x Stroke	Introduced	Used in
4988cc	84mm x 75mm	1987	E32 750i, 750iL
			E31 850i, 850Ci
5576cc	86mm x 80mm	1992	E31 850CSi

The M73 V12 engines, 1995 on

Further development of the M70 V12 engine produced the M73, which had both a larger bore and a longer stroke than the standard production M70 (and also differed in both dimensions from the Motorsport V12).

Capacity	Bore x Stroke	Introduced	Used in
5379cc	85mm x 79mm	1995	E38 750iL

There have also been some very special versions of the V12 engine, built for outside clients. Beginning in 1994, BMW's M Division built a 6064cc V12 known as the S70/2 type for the McLaren F1 supercar. This was a quad-cam, long-stroke version of the 5576cc engine and gave 627bhp. From 1997, there was also a shorter-stroke 5990cc version of the quad-cam V12 in the McLaren GTR. Then in 1998, BMW began supplying the 5379cc M73 V12 in slghtly modified 322bhp tune to Rolls-Royce for their new Silver Seraph saloon.

BMW's flagship engine is the V12

The BMW Story

SIX-CYLINDER DIESEL ENGINES

The M21 engines, 1985-1991

BMW started work on a diesel engine in the mid-Seventies, but production delays held things up until 1983. The engine was based on the M60 small-block petrol six, and shared several components with it. An indirect injection cylinder head was developed, and the first production versions were naturally aspirated; a turbocharged version followed two years later.

Capacity	Bore x Stroke	Introduced	Used in
2443cc	80mm x 81mm	1983	E30 324d
			E28 524d
2443cc (turbo)	80mm x 81mm	1985	E30 324td
			E28 524td

Versions of the M21 turbodiesel engine were supplied to Ford in the USA for the Lincoln Continental and MkVII models in 1983-1984, and to Bertone in Italy for the Freeclimber (based on the Daihatsu Fourtrak).

The M51 turbodiesel engine, 1991 to date

For the second-generation BMW six-cylinder diesel, the engine was redesigned with a longer stroke and a chain-driven camshaft. The basic configuration remained the same in other respects, however: indirect injection, an alloy cylinder head and cast-iron block, with a single overhead camshaft. This time, all versions were turbocharged, an intercooled engine being introduced before the less powerful non-intercooled type.

Capacity	Bore x Stroke	Introduced	Used in
2498cc	80mm x 82.8mm	1993	E36 325td
			E28 525td
2498cc (intercooled)	80mm x 82.8mm	1991	E36 325tds
			E34 525tds

Versions of the M51 turbodiesel engine are supplied to Opel for the Omega, and to Rover for the Range Rover.

The M57 turbodiesel engine, 1998 to date

The third-generation six-cylinder diesel uses common rail injection with a turbo-charger and intercooler. It is available in different states of tune to suit different models.

Capacity	Bore x Stroke	Introduced	Used in
2926cc	88.8mm x 84mm	1998	E39 530d
			E38 730d

Driving Machines

The M21 turbodiesel is seen here without its timing cover, showing the belt-drive to the camshaft...

...and in this picture with timing cover and cooling fan in place

The BMW Story

The M41 turbodiesel, 1994 to 1998

BMW's first four-cylinder diesel engine was developed directly from the M51 six-cylinder. It has been made available only in turbocharged and intercooled form.

Capacity	*Bore x Stroke*	*Introduced*	*Used in*
1665cc	80mm x 82.8mm	1994	E36 318tds

The M41 was BMW's first four-cylinder turbodiesel, and has now been replaced by the far more refined M47 type

The M47 turbodiesel engine, 1998 to date

BMW switched to common-rail direct injection for its second four-cylinder diesel engine. The M47 also had twin overhead camshafts and four valves per cylinder, together with a Variable Nozzle Turbine turbocharger and an intercooler.

Capacity	*Bore x Stroke*	*Introduced*	*Used in*
1951cc	88mm x 84mm	1998	E46 320d

A lower-powered version of this engine, known as the M47R, was supplied to Rover Group for use in the Rover 75 saloon from 1999.

Driving Machines

Index

Due to space constraints only the products of BMW and the companies of the BMW Group have been listed here.

Products of the BMW company

Aero engines: 007, 009, 015, 020, 025, 033, 036, 039, 040, 047, 112

Bicycles: 033

Cars : '02 models: 056, 059, 060, 061, 063, 065, 067, 068, 070, 075, 077, 078, 081
    3/15: 009, 013, 015, 016, 017, 023, 037
    3/20: 015, 016, 017, 021
    303: 015, 016, 017, 021
    309: 015, 016, 021
    315: 015, 017, 019, 021
    315/1 Roadster: 019, 021
    319: 015, 017, 018, 021, 026
    319/1 Roadster: 017, 019, 021, 026, 027
    320: 026, 029, 031
    321: 026, 031, 034, 037
    325: 030
    326: 023, 024, 026, 027, 029, 030, 031, 034, 037
    327: 024, 029, 031, 034, 036, 037
    327/28: 029, 031
    328: 024, 026, 027, 028, 029, 031, 034, 036, 037
    329: 026, 031
    331: 039
    332: 034
    335: 026, 030, 031
    340: 037
    503: 040, 047, 050, 051, 053, 056
    505: 040, 044
    507: 040, 047, 051, 052, 053
    600: 049, 053
    700 and LS: 047, 049, 050, 053, 055, 058, 076
    1600GT: 057
    1600ti: 060
    1700 (Glas): 057
    1800SA (1804): 057
    1800GL: 057
    2000C and CS: 061, 063, 066, 081
    2000SA (2004): 057
    3000: 057
    3200CS: 055, 056, 061, 063
    3 Series: 061, 067, 073, 075, 077, 078, 081, 094, 104, 111
        E21: 075, 076, 077, 078, 079
        E30: 077, 091, 093, 094, 095, 096, 097, 098, 099
        E36: 094, 101, 102, 103, 104, 109
        E46: 101, 103, 104

Index

5 Series: 067, 073, 074, 075, 077, 078, 081, 091, 111
      E12:   059, 073, 074, 075, 076, 078, 079, 083, 084, 092
      E28:   074, 078, 079, 086, 091, 092, 094, 096, 098, 099
      E34:   074, 078, 091, 092, 094, 096, 097, 098, 099
      E39:   101, 103, 104
6 Series:
      E24:   061, 067, 073, 081, 082, 083, 084, 086, 087, 089, 096, 102
7 Series: 067, 073, 081, 084, 102, 105, 111
      E23:   070, 081, 084, 085, 086, 089
      E32:   085, 094, 101, 109
      E38:   101, 103
8 Series:
      E31:   083, 101, 102, 111
E3:   065, 066, 067, 071, 074, 075, 081, 084
E9:   066, 068, 071, 078, 081, 082
M1:   070, 086, 087, 088, 089, 096
X5:   104
Z1:   101, 107, 109
Z3:   101, 107, 111
Z8:   107
Z13:   107
Baroque Angels: 039, 040, 041, 042, 043, 044, 045, 047, 048, 050, 052, 055, 056
Electric Cars: 106, 115
Gas Powered Cars: 106
Isetta: 040, 047, 048, 053, 055
New Class: 047, 055, 056, 058, 059, 060, 061, 063, 065, 067, 068, 073, 074

Motorcycles: 008, 009, 015, 025, 033, 034, 035, 039, 040, 047, 052, 062, 069, 088, 108, 113

BMW Group companies

BMW Motorsport GmbH: 067, 068, 073, 083, 107

BMW Rolls-Royce GmbH: 112

Kontron Elektronik GmbH: 114

Softlab GmbH: 114